WHEN EVERY HOUR'S A RUSH HOUR

Guilt Busters, Love Boosters, and Time-Savers

for Working Moms

WHEN EVERY HOUR'S A RUSH HOUR

Guilt Busters, Love Boosters, and Time-Savers

for Working Moms

by
Cristine B. Bolley and Joann C. Webster

Honor Books, Inc.
P. O. Box 55388
Tulsa, OK 74155

When Every Hour's a Rush Hour
ISBN 1-56292-056-1
Copyright © 1996 by Cristine B. Bolley and Joann C. Webster

Published by Honor Books, Inc.
P. O. Box 55388
Tulsa, OK 74155

DEDICATION

to all working mothers
and
to our families

Acknowledgments

Special thanks to Nikki Anderson and Gloria Kempton; and to Jo, Sonnie, Linda, Minette, Nancy, Patti, and Ruth, from whose stories, insights, and wisdom we gleaned to pass along to other working moms.

TABLE OF CONTENTS

Part II   A TIME TO RECEIVE

Dear Working Mom,

We are working mothers who have experienced the dilemma of dedication to both our careers and our homes. The "Rush Hour" prayer (page 17) was our own testimony of despair when we compared notes a few years ago. It also became our inspiration to find the answers which form this book.

When Cris was thirty years old, she gave birth to her first daughter. This happened just after she had found a job that could challenge and refine the skills she wanted to develop. Joann was thirty-five and well into her career when her children came to her by way of a judge's custody decision. We agree that the dedication to our work does not contain the intensity of purpose that inspires our devotion to our children. However, through exercising our skills at work we gain insight to give to the next generation. At home, we develop the generation who will value the wisdom gained through service to others. If a balance is found, the two passions can nourish each other, if unbalanced, one can destroy the other. Our children must always be our priority. But if time can be found for both our work inside and outside our home we can make a contribution to the world in which our children must live, and the benefits can contribute to our family's physical needs.

For many of us, a financial need in our family has forced us to find time to earn an income while raising our children. Balancing a budget is the practical side of life that doesn't question how we *feel* about working. But regardless of the reasons mothers work, the fact is, we do—which brings most of us into a conflict. When we do go to work, we feel guilty if we enjoy it and frustrated if we don't—so where can we find peace of mind?

As we searched for solutions to our dilemma, one of the biggest guilt busters we discovered was that the famous "Virtuous Woman" of Proverbs 31 earned an income in addition to raising her family. She made and sold garments, bought a field, and planted a vineyard. She worked so faithfully and dependably both outside and inside the home that her husband was known by *her* reputation. Where did this virtuous woman find balance?

King Solomon, who is remembered as the richest and wisest man in history, wrote his analysis of mankind's purpose on earth in his book, *Ecclesiastes*. He said that reverence for God and enjoyment of life is our only worthwhile pursuit, and that God's gift to mankind was for them to be glad, do good, and enjoy all the good of their labor. He also said there was a time to every purpose under heaven. *But,* we wondered, *where is the time to enjoy our labor?* As working mothers, we seldom have time to get our hair cut, let alone enjoy life!

We committed to look for answers to real-life situations that would free us from the frustrations we were experiencing. We determined to find truth that would balance us and give us clear direction once and for all. We talked to second-income moms, step-moms, and single moms and found that all breathed a sigh of relief as we discovered guilt busters together.

The most prevailing obstacle we uncovered was the lack of time. We each felt guilty that there wasn't enough time to attend to every person and task that needed our attention. We were surprised to learn that our stay-at-home grandmothers had the same obstacle of needing more time because their days were filled with household chores. Yet, when technology gave mothers time-saving gadgets, the extra time was often filled with more activities, not with more time for their children. This serves to illustrate that finding time for our children depends on how we *prioritize the time we have.* That's why this book is loaded with time-saving tips.

We found that both mothers who work at home and those who work outside the home share the common desire to find more time in each day. We examined many difficult situations that busy moms face and discovered that a simple prayer will keep us from losing precious time. By asking God to help us, we can avoid making mistakes that have to be redeemed. When mistakes have already been made, a simple prayer can quickly turn a trial into a triumph. The life builders at the end of the following stories are examples of prayers that can change us into virtuous women. Regardless of how painful the conflict was, we always found a nugget of truth deposited in the mother's life that could turn the sense of regret into a character-building opportunity. These nuggets are the beauty marks of their stories.

This book is a series of snapshots of working mothers' days and the guilt busters, time savers, and love boosters we found in their situations. The stories are true, but we used the names of our own children in place of the real names in order to protect both the innocent and the "guilty." (Plus it gave us the opportunity to thrill our families by using their names in a book.)

We hope you will read at least one story a week. They will help you learn to enjoy, as we have, the reward of work, womanhood, and the gift of time with your children.

In God's grace and power,

Cris and Joann

RUSH HOUR PRAYER

Lord, I love my family, I enjoy developing my creative skills, and the friendships I have made through my work enhance my life. But I have rooms that won't stay neat, a refrigerator that won't stay filled, floors that won't stay clean, and ironing I set aside so long ago that the children may have outgrown the clothes by now. There are boxes filled with good intentions under beds, hobbies in closets, and decorating items on shelves in the garage. No one claims ownership to any of it, and no one is authorized to throw it away. My children don't remember what "home-cooking" tastes like, and I can't even decide what restaurant to go to anymore.

I want to create special holiday memories this year. I want to teach my children how to enjoy life and grasp its fullness. I want to sit beside flowers in a garden, to hear the children's stories of what happens to them each day, and to be alone with my husband more often. I want to read the pile of books beside my bed and go shopping and have coffee with a friend. I need the gift of time to seek truths that will empower me with the knowledge to achieve my dreams.

I'm overwhelmed and I need to be rescued. God, please save me from this rush hour!

Guilt Buster Women have worked outside the home since time began. Some worked in their own gardens and some worked for others. Some were paid and some volunteered, but all had the opportunity to enjoy making a difference in the lives of people who knew them.

 Love Booster We can't control others but we can always influence them. Thank God for the opportunity to enrich someone else's life.

 Time Saver Learn to respond to life with love, and watch difficulties grow smaller and become more manageable.

 Life Builder *Lord, give me wisdom to build up my household, give me understanding to establish my family firmly, and give me knowledge to fill our memories with rare and beautiful treasures."*

"*By wisdom a house is built, and through understanding it is established; through knowledge its rooms are filled with rare and beautiful treasures.*"

Proverbs 24:3-4 NIV

PART ONE
A TIME TO GIVE

There is a time in a mother's life
when she can influence the choices
her children make.
This time is brief.
Her greatest inspiration to her
children is her own example
of making healthy choices that lead
to true happiness.
During this time of instruction,
a mother gives her child the courage
to move on.

Love Is

If I had the gift of being able to speak in other languages without learning them, and could speak in every language there is in all of heaven and earth, but didn't love others, I would only be making noise. If I had the gift of prophecy and knew all about what is going to happen in the future, knew everything about everything, but didn't love others, what good would it do? Even if I had the gift of faith so that I could speak to a mountain and make it move, I would still be worth nothing at all without love. If I gave everything I have to poor people, and if I were burned alive for preaching the Gospel but didn't love others, it would be of no value whatever.

Love is very patient and kind, never jealous or envious, never boastful or proud, never haughty or selfish or rude. Love does not demand its own way. It is not irritable or touchy. It does not hold grudges and will hardly even notice when others do it wrong. It is never glad about injustice, but rejoices whenever truth wins out. If you love someone you will be loyal to him no matter what the cost. You will always believe in him, always expect the best of him, and always stand your ground in defending him.

1 Corinthians 13:1-7 TLB

Women's Work

The corporate environment, with its politics and deadlines, weighed Nancy down. Every night she tried unsuccessfully to unwind during the drive home. The minute she arrived she marched into the kitchen, started dinner in her dress shoes, changed clothes as it cooked, then served her family.

She remained tense throughout dinner until the table shined and the dishwasher was running. Then she helped the kids with their homework, played with them, read to them, and tucked them into bed.

Her husband also worked for a large corporation. As they prepared for bed they shared a routine conversation. "I may have to work Sunday to catch up," he said.

"I wish I didn't have to work so I could spend more time with the children," Nancy moaned. "There just doesn't seem to be enough time."

"But we can't make it otherwise, Honey."

A weekend family picnic brought a welcome rest. Nancy's elderly grandmother came in a faded sun bonnet that looked as old and wrinkled as she did. "We work't ten hours in the field," grandmother recalled as Nancy lounged next to her. "Then we killt' a chick'n for dinner, 'n' made biscuits. Had to git up at four ever' day. But I like those store-bought biscuits. They're jis' about as good as mine."

Grandma rambled, mixing comments on old and new, until a thought formed in Nancy's mind. "When did you see your kids, Gramma?"

"What?" the older woman said laughing. "I had nine of 'em. Couldn't rem'ber their names ha'f the time! We work't ever' day but Sunday. The kids minded themselves most the time. Come to think of it, when the crops went bad we work't Sundays too. But these are the good days, with all our fancy kitchens, and we kin buy our veg'tibles at the mark't."

Nancy leaned over to her grandmother and kissed her cheek, excusing herself to join her children at the swing set.

"Push me, Mama," the girls cried almost in unison.

"Are you having fun?" Nancy asked cheerfully.

"Mommy, it's not time to leave is it?"

"No," Nancy said, "we have hours and hours."

Women have always worked hard and managed to raise good children, even in the "ole days."

 Affirm your children by occasionally breaking away from the adults to play with them.

 Turn time with your child into "quality time" simply by saying, "I'm sure glad we have this time together."

 Lord, help me to enjoy the privilege of raising my children and to worry less about the time it requires.

"Whatsoever things are true, whatsoever things are honest, whatsoever things are just, whatsoever things are pure, whatsoever things are lovely, whatsoever things are of good report; if there be any virtue, and if there be any praise, think on these things."

Philippians 4:8 KJV

Hey Mom, I'm home!

Lindsey wanted to become a "work-at-home mom" like her mother. As a kid, she loved entering through an unlocked door, knowing her mom was there. Even when she went to her friends' houses to play after school, her friends would shout greetings to let their mothers know they had arrived. Lindsey seldom saw the mothers, but she heard their voices from the kitchen, laundry room, den, or wherever work-at-home mothers were after school.

Since Lindsey's children were old enough for school, baby-sitters or grandparents most often greeted them instead of her. She talked with her children about how she wished she could be home after school, but she was also thankful for the benefits her family enjoyed from her work outside the home.

One day when Lindsey was grieving the loss of time with her children, she surprised everyone by coming home early. They surprised her by calling out to ask if they could go to a friend's house, promising to spend time with her later. After all, they had been studying all day, and it was sunny outside! "Good to see you, Mom. Talk to you later!" And they kissed her on the cheek before running out the unlocked door to meet their friends.

In the biographical movie *Shadowlands*, C.S. Lewis came to the conclusion that the grief we feel from being separated from certain people is an important part of the happiness we feel from being with them. We only miss being with those whom we truly love.

Guilt Buster

Even work-at-home moms will tell you that children are seldom found playing with their mothers after school.

Love Booster

Your children need you more at homework time (after dark) than when the sun is begging them to play.

Time Saver

Ask your children to explain to you what homework they have. Help them to allow enough time to finish their assignments before bedtime. Ask early enough to go to the store if extra supplies are needed for a special project.

Life Builder

Lord, help me to enjoy the good that comes from the work of my hands, and help my children to enjoy the good that comes from their homework too.

"A [woman] can do nothing better than to eat and drink and find satisfaction in [her] work. This too, I see, is from the hand of God, for without Him, who can eat or find enjoyment?"

Ecclesiastes 2:24-25 (author's paraphrase)

Team Fever

At Shelly's job, if you didn't work you didn't get paid, so she couldn't afford for her family to get sick.

When her oldest son woke up with a headache one morning, Shelly knelt by his bed and looked him in the eye.

"Please, can you try to get up? If you can go to school, Mommy can go to work and then we can buy groceries to eat." The little boy dragged himself out of bed and left for school. Whatever was ailing him lessened throughout the day. That night, to Shelly's relief, he felt fine.

Typically Shelly's kids didn't get sick like other children. She attributed that to good nutrition and to God's grace since she was a single mother trying to make a living. But one day at work, Shelly received a call from the school nurse saying her son was ill. When she arrived at the school to pick him up, the nurse said he had fainted in class from a high fever. Shelly crouched next to him where he lay on the cot in the nurse's office.

"Honey, why didn't you tell Mommy you didn't feel good this morning?"

"Because I wanted us to eat," he said.

Shelly was stricken with conscience and embarrassed over her circumstances as she looked up at the nurse. The nurse just smiled sympathetically.

That night after Shelly had gotten the fever under control and had tucked everyone in to bed, she lay awake questioning God why her son had to sacrifice himself just so she could make a living. Through the confusion of helplessness a single thought came to mind: *He is being a team player, just like you taught him.*

Shelly sat up in bed quietly pondering it. No, he didn't have the luxury of staying home whenever he felt like it, but he was building character as he worked toward a common goal with his mom. She laid back on her pillow once again, very proud of her son for doing what he thought was right even when it was hard.

Focus on what you *can* give your children instead of grieving over what you *can't* give them.

 Working together toward a common goal unites people—friends, colleagues, students, military, and family alike.

 Teach your kids to grade how bad they feel on a scale of one to ten to help you quickly decide what you will do. A headache is a "1," tonsillitis is a "10," etc.

 Thank you for strengthening us, protecting us, healing us, and giving us our daily bread.

"For you yourselves know how you ought to follow our example. We were not idle when we were with you, nor did we eat anyone's food without paying for it. On the contrary, we worked night and day, laboring and toiling so that we would not be a burden to any of you. We did this, not because we do not have the right to such help, but in order to make ourselves a model for you to follow. For even when we were with you, we gave you this rule: 'If a man will not work, he shall not eat.' And...never tire of doing what is right."

—Paul, Apostle to the Church

2 Thessalonians 3:7-11,13

Burnt Offerings

Erin's daughter began her usual table grace, "Dear Lord, thank You for this food, and bless the one who prepared it." Then she added," and bless Daddy who kept it from burning. Amen." Instead of wincing Erin smiled. She knew that whether it was haute cuisine or hot dogs, her children would remember the time they spent together at the family table more than her lack of cooking skills.

Erin's husband disliked burnt food enough to help her with the cooking. When he heard a lid rattle on the waterless cookware, he hurried to the kitchen. The waterless cookware was another one of Erin's purchases intended to increase her enjoyment of cooking. She bought every kitchen gadget she could afford—the new miracle thaw plate, a battery operated carrot peeler, a butter cutter, an apple corer, a garlic press, and a pepper grinder. Most nights, she had everything but the groceries.

Erin avoids the food-gathering ritual of going to the grocery store, yet she wants her family around the table as often as possible. When they tire of deciding between burnt food and noisy restaurants, they bring carry-out meals to their home. When given the choice of the breakfast room or the dining room, Erin's daughter prefers to set the formal dining table.

Through her child's actions Erin saw that the gathering of the family, not the food, was what they desperately craved. Immediately her guilt over not cooking ended. Around their own table they slowed down and shared stories they had heard. Sometimes they discussed new words they had learned or planned upcoming weekends together.

In Old Testament days, food sacrifices were brought to the temple. The burnt offerings for trespasses were consumed by fire on the altar. The fellowship offering, however, was for thanksgiving and was eaten together with the priest.

While our kitchen stovetops may sometimes produce burnt offerings, our dining tables can still become altars of thankfulness for food eaten together. It is the fellowship we share, not the salt and pepper, that flavors our meals.

 **Guilt Buster** Children need to eat meals with family members. Home-*eaten* meals matter more than home-*cooked* meals.

 Love Booster Encourage your family to linger at the table by asking them questions that show your interest in what happened to them that day.

 Time Saver Buy a few heat-and-serve meals to keep on hand for nights you are especially tired.

 Life Builder *Lord, thank You for our daily food and fellowship.*

*"He who brings an offering of praise
and thanksgiving honors and glorifies Me; and
he who orders his way aright—who prepares the way
that I may show him—to him I will demonstrate
the salvation of God."*

Psalm 50:23 AMP

One-Armed Solutions

Lecture followed lecture, but Jamie was at a loss for a way to impress upon her teenage sons the necessity of cleaning. They just didn't "get" cleanliness, preferring instead to dirty every inch of their clothes, pollute their bathroom, and pile dirty dishes wherever they happened to be eating.

One night during dinner, one of the boys told the family about his class theme paper on empathizing with the handicapped. First he talked about blindness, and both boys tried to eat with their eyes closed. Later he put one arm inside his shirt to show how a person with a missing arm would have to eat. His brother quickly followed suit.

Near the end of dinner, Jamie had an idea and ran upstairs to put on a T-shirt. When everyone was finished eating, she pulled her arm inside her shirt too, and announced, "Okay, it's time for one-arm clean-up."

The boys enthusiastically joined in. Two of them had to work together to scrape the plates with one holding and the other scraping. Two were needed to store leftovers. The only thing they could do alone was clear the table, which was quickly accomplished.

Eventually they gave up and finished the task with both hands and a lively conversation. "Ooh, that would be horrid to have only one arm." "Every day we should be thankful we're healthy." "Does Uncle Guy really just have one eye...."

Soon the kitchen was sparkling and the boys were cheerful and happy when they started their homework. Jamie was happy too. She had discovered a way to get the boys to help, and they even enjoyed themselves in the process.

The next night just before clean-up time, Jamie asked the boys to retell their favorite movies to her. Again, they scarcely noticed they were cleaning. The following nights topics ranged from cars to study hall to science—anything that interested the boys. Jamie's solution didn't directly train her children to be clean, but it did reduce her frustration in motivating them toward it.

Guilt Buster "You can't mold clay when it's dry." We can't achieve the goals we have for our kids without their participation, so sometimes we have to wait.

 **Love Booster** Creating a fun environment makes any chore easier.

 Time Saver Rally the family together as a team, even if they don't always understand or do things perfectly.

 Life Builder *Please show me the secrets and shortcuts I'll need to meet the challenges of this day.*

"Train up a child in the way he should go: and when he is old, he will not depart from it."

Proverbs 22:6 KJV

Clean Your Room or Eat My Cooking

"Are the gum wrappers on your bedroom floor for a reason?" Lindsey complained to her daughter. "And I've told you to hang up your clothes so we won't have so much laundry to do." The girl's room looked like Lindsey's room had when she was twelve, yet Lindsey still lectured her about the need to be organized and self-motivated. Careless words took an angry aim. "How can you live in this mess?!"

"Chill out, Mom. Just go away. I'll clean it up." The girl's voice was sharp with hurt. Lindsey knew that leaving the room was a good option, but she was already full of regret by the time she reached the hallway outside her daughter's door. She hadn't intended to criticize her daughter—again. *Help me, Lord, to start this conversation over,* she silently prayed. Lindsey's daughter didn't look up as she reentered the room.

"I'm sorry," Lindsey said to her. "I really came in to find out if you need help with your homework." She could see that her daughter wasn't ready to talk. "Because if you do," Lindsey continued, "I might let Dad off kitchen duty so he can help you."

The girl finally smiled, "Does that mean *you* would cook dinner instead of him? No thanks, Mom. I'm too hungry to give up his good cooking!" They both laughed and Lindsey's daughter opened up to her again. As she listened to her daughter's campaign plans for class treasurer, Lindsey picked up the gum wrappers and threw them in the trash can. Her daughter didn't even notice when Lindsey hung up the clothes that had been tossed on the chair.

They decided to make campaign necklaces instead of buttons, so Lindsey agreed to take her daughter out for supplies when she finished her homework. As they talked, Lindsey put away sweaters and jeans. This time when Lindsey left her daughter's room *it* looked better to *her* and *she* looked better to her *daughter.*

 Parenting is about setting an example, not demanding a result.

 It only takes a few minutes to clear the clutter that blocks the view of your love for someone.

 Instead of focusing on instruction, praise the qualities you most admire in your children and exemplify the qualities you want them to develop.

 Lord, let the words of my mouth be acceptable in Your sight and delightful to the ears of my children.

"Therefore, as God's chosen people, holy and dearly loved, clothe yourselves with compassion, kindness, humility, gentleness and patience. Bear with each other and forgive whatever grievances you have against one another. Forgive as the Lord forgave you."

Colossians 3:12-13

Vacuum Ready

One job was bad enough, but two brought new trials to Nancy's home. Her second job was speculative—a career in music. She had started it years earlier, before her conversion to Christianity. Now she wanted to use her talent for God.

Her first obstacle was carving out time for practices and the few performances that she had booked. Then came the financial drain for equipment and a recording she could sell. The last step was publicity.

Each step meant new sacrifices for Nancy's young daughters, who didn't notice any changes until Nancy assigned chores. Nancy didn't have the time to do all she had been doing before. "You will have to clean your rooms yourself," Nancy informed them. She inspected their rooms an hour later only to find toys and clothes still strewn on the floor. Nancy flew into exasperated fits for weeks until she realized they didn't fully understand the concept of "clean."

"Get everything off the floor so it's vacuum-ready," Nancy patiently explained. "I will vacuum your rooms after I've vacuumed the rest of the house. When you hear the vacuum coming near your door you will only have a few minutes to finish cleaning."

When she arrived at the first room with the vacuum cleaner, she found the floor clear, although the bed and dresser still warranted some work. The second was the same. After mastering vacuum-ready, the girls soon learned dusting-ready, dishwasher-ready, and laundry-ready.

With her time better prioritized, Nancy has only to garner the hard-sought concert invitations. Her dream does not diminish and her girls' willingness to help does not waver. As Nancy's little team perseveres, they are learning how to find time one day for their own dreams.

Guilt Buster

The sacrifice your family makes to help you follow your dream may not be as big as you think.

 Love Booster

Explain what you want from others and watch peace prevail over chaos. Solutions are more effective than blame.

 Time Saver

"Something-ready" is a term easy enough for children to understand. When the children clean their rooms, ask if it is "inspection-ready." Always praise them when you see they have made a notable effort, even if there is still room for improvement.

 Life Builder

Lord, help me be open to You when You come to clean my heart.

"But when the kindness and love of God our Savior appeared, he saved us, not because of righteous things we had done, but because of his mercy. He saved us through the washing of rebirth and renewal by the Holy Spirit, whom he poured out on us generously through Jesus Christ our Savior."

Titus 3:4-6

"Save Time, See it My Way"

"It's not fair!" shouted Erin's angry seven-year-old. Erin wondered what new injustice her older children had dealt to her youngest. When her daughter finally stopped shouting long enough to present her case to Erin's council and jury, the story was the usual—her sisters wouldn't let her play with them.

"What do you want me to do about it?" Erin asked her.

"Make them be nice to me," she sobbed.

Erin wanted to read books to her daughter that had impacted her own life. Dale Carnegie's *How To Win Friends and Influence People* (Pocket Books, NY, NY) would be an apropos beginning. She wanted to exchange her daughter's bedtime story with William Lantz's book, *The 51% Principle* (Honor Books, Tulsa, OK), so her daughter would understand people can't *control* other people's actions; they can only *influence* them. Other people can influence us, but they can't *make* us do anything we aren't *willing* to do. We have fifty-one percent control over our own response to what others ask us to do; we have a forty-nine percent potential of influencing others. Erin wanted her daughter to learn to influence people so she could become a success. But her daughter was too young to understand, so Erin reached for God's wisdom.

"Sweetheart," she said, "I can't make them do what you want, but it will make your heart feel better if you forgive them." Dissatisfied with that answer, the little girl stomped off to her room. Feeling deflated and defeated, Erin let the situation go.

The next day Erin's older daughter surprised her by saying, "Mom, you have given us the secret to happiness."

"I have?" Erin replied. "And what's that?"

"You have taught us to forgive each other. Not many of my friends at school seem to like their brothers or sisters. I wish everyone knew how to forgive others."

Erin hugged her daughter and decided to persevere with teaching her younger daughter the basic principles of success.

Guilt Buster

We may not be able to keep our children from fighting, and we may not have the best answer every time, but we can teach our children how to make up with each other, which is one of life's most important lessons.

 Love Booster

Teach your children to do what is right, regardless of what others are doing. Forgiveness is a great medicine for any heart.

 Time Saver

When you are groping for guidance for the right thing to do in a situation, choose what love would do.

 Life Builder

Lord, help me to think of ways to show forgiveness instead of ways to get even with those who offend me.

"A righteous man may have many troubles, but the Lord delivers him from them all."

Psalm 34:19

Play Pays

Jamie had too much to do on her day off. Her husband had to work a weekend shift, leaving her alone to handle all the errands. She laid in bed going over the list in her head, wondering how she would ever get it all done. Then she forced herself to get out of bed and headed downstairs.

Her teenage son, Mark, lay sprawled across the couch channel surfing. Their relationship was strained, and seeing his laziness surfaced fresh resentment. However, instead of giving in to her frustrations, Jamie sat down on the other couch.

"Whatcha watching?"

"Nothin'," he said, glancing at her. He looked sweet and young lying there, incapable of mischief or anger toward her.

Abruptly she said, "Do you want to go to breakfast?"

He looked at her for a moment. "Sure."

Jamie instantly felt the crush of time and regretted the offer. "Okay, I'll get ready," she said impulsively, before she could change her mind. As she showered and dressed, a sense of fun rolled away some of the dark clouds.

"What's been going on with you?" Mark asked as they were seated at the restaurant.

She answered, then asked about him. He told her about his girlfriend, his car, and his job. He was intent on changing jobs, which distressed her, but she kept quiet.

"We need groceries," she said as they finished eating.

"Let's go," he offered. "I'll help shop."

Working together, they whisked through the shopping, then raced home. "Can you put away the groceries while I start the laundry?" she asked. He agreed, then went out to wash his car while she cleaned indoors.

"Would you wash mine, too?" Jamie called to him.

By the end of the afternoon she sat in the clean living room sorting through her household bills. Mark brought his few bills downstairs and asked about making a budget, something Jamie had been wanting to teach him. When they finished, he headed out for an evening with his friends.

"I've been thinking," he said as he walked out the door, "I guess I'll keep my job for now. Bye!"

Jamie made dinner and left his portion wrapped in the refrigerator with a big note, "Thanks for such a nice day."

We don't always have to say *no* to fun and *yes* to duty. Spontaneity is the spice of life.

 The only bad day is the day we spend more time on things than people.

 Enlist others' help by saying, "I'd love for you to do this or go there with me," instead of making it a chore.

 Give me the wisdom and knowledge to know when to speak up and when to just pray.

"A gentle answer turns away wrath, but a harsh word stirs up anger."

Proverbs 15:1

Creating Heroes

Byron rushed from his Sunday school class, exuberantly babbling to his mother, Ashley, about his standing in the Bible contest. Her once-reluctant Sunday schooler was now seriously reading his Bible during the week, memorizing Scripture, and dragging the family out of bed early on Sunday mornings.

Byron's teacher stood smiling in the doorway watching him tell his mother about his victory. Ashley's heart swelled with appreciation for all his teacher had done to help train her son. She considered inviting her to dinner, but instantly dismissed the idea like she had every Sunday before. With lessons, sports, homework, and trying to keep up with her own friends, she didn't need another busy evening entertaining someone she barely knew.

Then Ashley remembered when her parents had invited T. "Texas" Tyler to dinner when she was five years old. She had tried to brag about this "premier event" for years but never found anyone who had heard of him. Still, the ignorance of her friends never tarnished the splendor of his memory. She couldn't recall his face, but she remembered the old stereo record he had left behind and his story: He had been a rising star in country music but gave it up to sing in little churches like the one she was now attending. The impression that came to mind year after year was of a man who gave up everything to follow Jesus.

Ashley's thoughts jumped to a typical evening at home. After she disposed of dirty dishes she normally slumped into a kitchen chair to catch up on paperwork and listen to marginally tasteful sitcoms her children watched in the family room. Ashley moved forward to intercept Byron's teacher who was preparing to leave.

When Byron heard that his teacher was coming to dinner, he dashed off to boast to his friends about his upcoming "premier event."

It doesn't take a clean house, great food, or a world-famous celebrity to create a lasting impression on a child.

 Create a "T. 'Texas' Tyler" experience for your children by inviting their heroes to dinner. Little league coaches, Sunday school teachers, and kind-hearted neighbors all make great candidates for positive role models for your children.

 When you can't invite their heroes to dinner, be sure to tell stories to your children about godly, heroic people so they will learn to look for virtuous characteristics in others.

 Lord, thank You for sending heroes to set examples for my children.

"I want the company of the godly men and women in the land; they are the true nobility."

Psalm 16:3 TLB

Managing Hormones

"Mom, I'm in love," her 15-year-old exclaimed breathlessly as Jamie walked in the door from work.

"Really?" she asked, setting down a bag of groceries on the kitchen counter. "Who is it this week?"

"Mom, I'm serious," he said. "She really is the girl for me."

"But if you just started liking her, you don't even know her yet."

"I do too know her," he said defensively, "Her name's Jillian!"

Jamie squelched a laugh. As she cooked dinner, she realized the infatuations and crushes of pre-teen years had given way to her son's hormones. She worried that these early relationships could hurt him if she didn't somehow protect him. That night Jamie told her husband that she would like to start taking their sons out one at a time, so they could learn how to date, and know what to look for in a girl. He agreed to entertain the son she didn't take out.

The dating began. With one son or the other, Jamie showed them how to enjoy the best Thai food in the area, the free silent movies at the museum, and the best open-air concerts. They had their low points, one of them got sick watching a 360° movie, and the other got sick from too much garlic while trying escargot. But all their experiences created cherished memories and a vast reservoir of impressions.

Jamie was proud of how her sons behaved like gentlemen. She knew they could recognize a girl who acted like a lady. The evenings together didn't spare the boys the painful task of reaching adulthood. They still suffered all the ups and downs of normal kids. Then, two years after leaving home, her oldest son called from his apartment.

"Mom," he said, "when does the Shakespeare festival start?"

Jamie told him and smiled inwardly. *If he's found a girl who shares his faith and also likes Shakespeare,* she thought, *he's probably found a nice girl.*

Guilt Buster

Basically, by the time your children are teenagers, they are raised. From then on, you can't control them, but you can influence them by showing them how to make good choices.

 Love Booster

Creating memories is important. Take pictures of everyday happenings and special events, collect matchbooks from restaurants you visit, or put together scrapbooks with tickets to cultural events and amusement parks. Use them to remind your family of the loving times you have shared.

 Time Saver

Get on the mailing lists of museums, symphonies, or theaters so you can be educated about what is happening in your community.

 Life Builder

Please prepare the person my child will marry. Give them a heart after You and good character, and let them love my child as much as I do.

"Love the Lord your God with all your heart and with all your soul and with all your strength. These commandments that I give you today are to be upon your hearts. Impress them on your children. Talk about them when you sit at home and when you walk along the road, when you lie down and when you get up."

Deuteronomy 6:5-7

And the Katydid Sang!

Hunting insects for her daughter's science project wasn't exactly how Lindsey wanted to spend her Saturday afternoon. Her chores at home had piled up, she was exhausted from the week's work, and she looked forward to easing the pressure by cleaning house.

"But Mother, it could be fun," her daughter said enthusiastically. "Dad will help and we could have a picnic in the park. I have to find eight different kinds of insects by Monday but I only have the katydid we caught yesterday. Do you think I should poke holes in the lid?" she asked, looking at the bug in the jar.

"Not if you plan to pin him to a Styrofoam block tomorrow," Lindsey replied, crossing the room to look more closely at this light green cousin to the grasshopper. A week ago there would not have been a problem catching bugs for the project, but an early frost nipped the easy catches. However, the elegant bug in long coattails was a great specimen for her assignment.

Suddenly, the katydid sounded like it was playing miniature Mexican maracas inside the jar. The more familiar sounds of crickets responded through the open window. The katydid's clatter together with the cricket's cadence sounded like a tiny rhythm band. The katydid led the twilight jubilation, waving his antennas in perfect meter like a conductor's baton.

"The katydid is singing." Lindsey's daughter whispered with delight. To Lindsey it sounded like he was praising God. "I want to set it free," the girl said quietly.

Lindsey looked at her daughter and saw tears, but couldn't tell if they were in her eyes or her daughter's. Lindsey knew that her daughter's tender heart and gentle spirit were worth far more than an A+ on her science project.

"Then you must let it go," Lindsey told her, "I'll make sandwiches for our picnic tomorrow. You're right. I think it will be fun to hunt for bugs together." Looking again at the inspiring katydid, she added, "But I hope the bugs we find are ugly."

Guilt Buster

A child-like perspective, creativity, curiosity, and compassion are great tools for handling pressures.

 Love Booster

Weekends are short, and childhood is fleeting, so picnic while you can.

 Time Saver

On orientation night at your child's school, find out what science projects your child will be expected to complete. Encourage your child to start early so you won't have to fight the forces of nature to meet the deadline.

 Life Builder

Lord, help me to learn from the katydid, whose days were lengthened by praising You.

"And if thou wilt walk in my ways, to keep my statutes and my commandments...then I will lengthen thy days."

1 Kings 3:14 KJV

"Hold Me, I'm Growing!"

Ashley took as much time off from work as possible while her babies were small. Many well-meaning homemakers told her the rules about naps, bottles, and baby care. But her sister-in-law, Jane, gave her the best advice, "Hold them as much as you can because they will soon be grown and want off your lap." Ashley trusted Jane because she had already raised eight children who each had a tender love for her. True, the goal of parenting is to prepare a child to leave one day, but that day seemed a long way off when Ashley's first baby was placed in her arms.

In those early weeks of motherhood when Ashley's husband left for work in the morning she was already holding their baby. When he arrived home at night she was still holding their baby. She decided that if she was going to feel guilty about doing the wrong thing, she wanted to feel guilty about holding her babies too much. In time she had to let them go. As her sister-in-law predicted, each baby wanted loose far sooner than she tired of holding them.

A Time To Give

Ashley's children want to spend more and more time away from home now. After all, her oldest child is thirteen. Soon they will take their final steps to independence, but Ashley is holding on to them a bit longer. She reminds them that in only a few precious years, a driver's license will grant them greater independence. And she has many things left to teach them about adult responsibilities.

Even though to them their teen years will seem to last forever, Ashley can see the years will seem too short to her. Ashley knows her creative work can wait, but her growing children can't. To be with them during these pivotal years, Ashley regularly turns down business trips that could promote her career. As she explains to her boss, "Knowing the goal is to set my children free, I have to invest myself in them now."

Guilt Buster

It's okay to hold a baby, and later to say no to a child who is on the go too much.

 Love Booster

Be sure to explain why you say no to privileges that your child is requesting. Understanding boundaries builds a firm foundation.

 Time Saver

Treat your pre-teen children like small adults and schedule times to train each one for more adult responsibilities. Explain that you want to prepare them for being on their own. You may begin with household tasks and move to personal planning skills, such as goal setting and checkbook maintenance. (See page 98 for more suggestions.)

 Life Builder

Lord, instruct me in the way I should train my children so their steps will not be hampered, and they will run and not stumble.

"Take fast hold of instruction; let her not go: keep her;
for she is thy life."

Proverbs 4:13 KJV

Duty Calls

It was all Erin could do to keep her own household together but when her sister, a mother of two, ended up in jail after a tumultuous teenage life, Erin knew there was just one thing to do. She moved her nephews, ages five and seven, into her home and faced the difficulties head-on.

The boys had no appetite for proper nourishment after being raised on junk food. They were behind in school, had no social skills, and were mystified by personal hygiene. The first day Erin dropped them off at the baby-sitter's on her way to work, one sat in a chair all day, refusing to eat, talk, or play.

Erin's youngest daughter resented them, refused to give up her bedroom, and protested when it was suggested the boys call her parents "Mom and Dad." Being the youngest, it was understandable that she didn't want to give up her position.

Erin and her husband spent evenings attacking the problems one by one. Erin refused to cook separate meals for different family members and concentrated on the most palatable foods possible to lure her new charges into a balanced diet. Her husband helped with their hygiene. The older children pitched in to teach homework and house rules, reluctantly at first but then with joy as they saw change. The advantages the girls had over their cousins soon became apparent even to them and their increasing compassion for the little boys caused the girls to grow in unexpected strides.

Erin was often tempted to quit her job but even though it was stressful, she knew her income was even more helpful to their family now. There were two more children to feed, clothe, and educate, not to mention two more sets of teeth to straighten. Two years later, the boys looked like Erin's own children. They had a strong resemblance to her daughters and shared family memories and values that made them fit. For Erin, what started as duty turned to love. Now, when Erin kisses the four clean faces goodnight, raising children isn't any less work, but it seems more fulfilling.

Guilt Buster Not everyone can add needy children to their family, but we can appreciate those who do.

 Love Booster Each person in a family multiplies the amount of love available to spread between its members.

 Time Saver When older children help younger ones with their homework, it reinforces the older child's knowledge and strengthens the bond between them.

 Life Builder *Open my eyes to what I can share with the less fortunate, and to the benefits I have taken for granted.*

"Then shall the righteous answer [Jesus], saying, Lord, when saw we thee an hungred, and fed thee?...or naked, and clothed thee? And the King shall answer and say unto them, Verily I say unto you, Inasmuch as ye have done it unto one of the least of these my brethren, ye have done it unto me."

Matthew 25:37-38,40 KJV

Sweet Dreams

Shelly's fifteen-year-old son asked in his no-longer-a-boy-baritone, "Mom, will you pray with me?" She smiled and followed him to his room while her mind flashed back through the years.

The vision of him in footie pajamas running and sliding into bed across a linoleum floor flitted across her mind. She remembered how when he was small he prayed in her arms, and the warm feeling that came with those cozy nights still felt fresh. His prayers back then went something like: "Please give me a tricycle for Christmas," or "Heal the ow-ee on my finger," or "Bless Gramma and Grampa."

Shelly vaguely remembered more formal prayers from her own childhood and was happy that her son knew how to speak honestly to God. She fully expected the tradition of bedtime prayers to end around the time her children no longer asked to be tucked in. Instead, she had instilled something within them that was more than a routine before a good-night kiss.

The young man's prayers were filled with thank-yous and practical requests about tomorrow's responsibilities, ideas for an essay, and a solution to a job problem, as well as some needs of his friends and family. Shelly prayed after him. "Father, I agree with my son for these things to be done in the name of Your wonderful Son, Jesus Christ."

She left his room, sensing God's power in their prayer, and felt a deep gratitude toward the Lord. When she said her prayers that night, she thanked God that her children had outgrown favorite blankets and stuffed toys, baby talk and thumb sucking, but not their childlike faith in Him.

Guilt Buster We see God best with our eyes closed. Your children won't always listen to you, but they will most likely imitate you.

 **Love Booster** More is accomplished by two knees bowed in prayer than by two legs frantic in busyness.

 **Time Saver** Buy a book of children's bedtime prayers to use on nights when your mind is weary.

 Life Builder *Lord, help me teach my children that we never out grow bedtime prayers.*

*"If two of you shall agree on earth as touching
any thing that they shall ask, it shall be done for them of
my Father which is in heaven."*

Matthew 18:19 KJV

☺

Wake Up Calls

It seemed like Jamie just couldn't get enough sleep. With two handsome sons, and girls being as forward as they were, the telephone was always ringing at their house. The rule was, "No calls after 9:00 pm," but that was stretched often.

Finally, when the calls started coming after midnight, Jamie made a new rule: If your friend calls and wakes me up, you get grounded. Surprisingly the calls, which the boys had insisted they had no control over, stopped.

A few months later Jamie was thrilled when her oldest son started driving. He was eager to run errands and provide taxi service for his younger brother. All those sports practices and Friday-night church activities for the youth were now opportunities for Jamie to have a quiet, peaceful evening at home.

Jamie's husband administered curfews gently. If you couldn't make curfew, call home, but call by 9:00. It worked, since not complying meant not using Mom and Dad's car again. But then the inevitable happened. Her son bought his own car.

Once his sense of independence and self-confidence broadened, he called later and later. Many mornings Jamie dragged herself out of bed to get to work without enough sleep. After a stern talk, her

son did better. Yet some calls seemed justified—flat tires, getting lost, losing keys, running out of gas, or needing to give a ride home to a friend who was stranded.

Night after night Jamie was awakened by the shrill ring and the familiar, "Mom?" *Why does he always pose it as a question?* she thought impatiently. *Who does he think would answer the phone?* The continued interruption of sleep was like having a newborn in the house again, only this sleepless dependent was 6'4" tall and eighteen years old.

After dozens of talks and many precious hours of sleep lost, Jamie's son moved out to find his own way in life. It was the end of an era. Jamie cried when he left and reminded him to call if he needed anything. Then she went to bed and slept soundly.

Guilt Buster No home is perfect, no child always follows the rules, and no mother always gets eight hours of sleep a night.

 Love Booster Living through a teenager's immaturity is often more trying than diapers and colic, yet the reward in the end is just as great.

 Time Saver When your kids become teenagers with busy evenings, a cat nap after work takes the edge off responding to the late-night needs in your teenager's life.

 Life Builder *Thank You. Lord, for answering every time I call, and for being my strength even in my weakness.*

"This is what the Lord says, he who made the earth, the Lord who formed it and established it—the Lord is his name: 'Call to me and I will answer you and tell you great and unsearchable things you do not know.'"

Jeremiah 33:2-3

More Time-Saver Tips:

MENU PLANNING MAKES MEALS AT HOME EASIER

It only takes a few minutes longer to plan four weeks of meals than it does to plan for seven days. Fill in a thirty-day meal-planning menu once a month, then when you are ready to shop for groceries you can check the menu for the items you need for that trip to the store.

Ask family members to give you a list of their favorite meals. Write their ideas on index cards from which you can select future menus. Make a separate card for each category of meat or entree. Your categories may include a card for beef, chicken, pork, soup or casserole suggestions. As you try new recipes, add the name of the entrees you like to the appropriate index card. Soon you will be able to plan two or three months of meals at a time without repeating the menu.

When planning meals, start with one or two vegetables you want to serve, then add varying choices of entrees—poultry, fish, or low-fat beef. Potatoes, rice, breads, beans, and legumes are also counted as a main entree and can be substituted for a meat dish. Be sure to offer your family plenty of fresh fruit in the morning and as snacks throughout the day. See Harvey and Marilyn

Diamond's book *Fit for Life*, (Warner Books, New York, NY) for more ideas on healthy meals to feed your family.

Keep an index card with reminders of events or schedules around which you must plan your meals, such as sporting events and music lessons. Save complicated meals and new recipes for nights when you have plenty of time.

Here is a sample schedule:

MENU SCHEDULE

Sunday: choose a slow-cooker or oven meal that can cook during church

Monday: choose a soup or casserole that can use Sunday's leftovers

Tuesday: buy groceries and bring home fresh fish from the market

Wednesday: busy schedule—eat out

Thursday: house cleaning night—choose simple family favorites, then clean together

Friday: everyone is home—try new recipes—invite friends

Saturday: picnics or backyard meals

Post the menu plan on the kitchen bulletin board or refrigerator where family members can see it. Whoever is first to arrive home can check the menu and start the meal.

When Every Hour's a Rush Hour

The following is a sample menu:

24 MEALS YOUR FAMILY CAN START BEFORE YOU GET HOME

SUN	MON	TUE	WED	THUR	FRI	SAT
Sweet Potatoes Ham	Ham & Bean Soup with Cornbread	Sautéed Zucchini Breaded Fish Rice	Eat Out	Spaghetti Salad	Hamburger Macaroni Casserole*	Corn on the cob Hamburgers
Rice/Peas Baked Chicken	Chicken Noodle Soup & Toasted French Bread	Peas Tuna Helper	Eat Out	Taco Salad	Creamed Tuna*	Spinach Barbecue Pork Chops
Mashed Potatoes Green Beans Roast	Vegetable Beef Soup & Biscuits	Asparagus Salmon Patties	Eat Out	Lasagna	Mexican Casserole*	Rueben Sandwiches
Baked Potato Salad Grilled Steak	Potato Soup	Green Beans Steamed Fish	Eat Out	Enchiladas	Snake 'n Beans*	Okra Oven-fried Chicken Strips

*Recipe follows

Keep a copy of each calendar to recycle in the future.

A Time To Give

MEALS ON THE RUN recipes
even your children can make

(Also known as "No Brainer" Cooking)

For meals with little preparation and quick clean up, try these:

HAMBURGER MACARONI CASSEROLE

Serves 4 big eaters

Shopping: Approximately 1 lb. hamburger

      1 box macaroni and cheese

      1 can mushroom soup

Preheat oven to 350°. Brown hamburger. Meanwhile, prepare macaroni and cheese according to package directions. When the hamburger is nicely browned (no longer pink), drain it and add to the macaroni and cheese. Add the mushroom soup and mix well. Pour into a casserole dish or 13" x 9" cake pan and bake at 350° for 10-20 minutes (depending on how much time you have).

Note: You may want to use ground round. It's lower in fat than the average hamburger meat, but it's less expensive than ground sirloin, which is lowest in fat.

FOR A COMPLETE MEAL:

While the casserole bakes, cook some vegetables on the stove, pop some brown-and-serve rolls in the oven (with the casserole), and pour individual bowls of apple sauce. The casserole, veggies, and rolls will all be ready to serve at the same time.

CREAMED TUNA

Serves 2 big eaters

Shopping: 1 can tuna

1 can mushroom soup

bread

Stir tuna with mushroom soup in saucepan. When mixture is hot, make toast. Pour tuna mixture over toast and serve immediately.

FOR A COMPLETE MEAL:

While tuna mixture cooks, make a hearty salad with fresh lettuce, tomatoes, carrots, and anything else you have handy. Preset salad and dressings on the table so the creamed tuna can be served hot.

MEXICAN CASSEROLE

Serves 4 big eaters

Shopping: Approximately 1 lb. hamburger

1 pkg. taco seasoning

1 can crescent roll dough

1 cup shredded cheddar cheese

Preheat oven to 350°. Brown hamburger in a skillet. Add taco seasoning. While meat is browning, press crescent roll dough flat in bottom of 13" x 9" cake pan. Bake about 5 minutes. Pour meat over half-baked croissant dough. Sprinkle with cheese. Bake 15 minutes.

FOR A COMPLETE MEAL:

Slice fresh cucumber, carrots, and celery while casserole cooks. Set on the table with a bowl of corn chips. Serve casserole piping hot.

SNAKE 'N BEANS

Serves 6 big eaters

Shopping: 1 lb. beef or chicken, cut in strips

2 Tbs. oil

1 onion, chopped

2 16 oz. packages frozen green beans

(optional: green pepper, celery, or 2 packages of your favorite mixed vegetables can be added or substituted.)

1 can mushrooms, drained, liquid reserved

Heat oil in skillet. Add meat and brown until no longer pink. Add onion and beans and sauté 3 to 5 minutes until onion is soft and beans are crisp-tender. To reserved mushroom liquid, add 1 Tbs. soy sauce and enough water to make 1 cup. Mix with cornstarch until smooth. Add to skillet with mushrooms. Cook until the liquid is clear.

FOR A COMPLETE MEAL:

Serve with rice.

APPLE CRUMBLE

Serves 6 big eaters

Shopping: 1 white cake mix

1 stick butter

1 can apple pie filling

Preheat oven to 350°. Pour apple pie filling into 13" x 9" cake pan. Sprinkle entire cake mix on top. Dot the top of the cake mix with very thin pats of butter (use more or less depending on taste). Bake for 20 minutes or until brown. Serve hot with ice cream, if desired. (For another delicious dessert, substitute a yellow cake mix and can of peaches, and sprinkle with 1 cup each of shredded coconut and pecans.)

GROCERY LISTS MADE EASY — So Someone Else Can Go For You

Group foods together on your grocery list as they are found in the aisles of the store you most often visit to make it easier for other family members to shop for you. It also keeps you from backtracking at the market when you are in hurry.

FRESH PRODUCE	CANNED GOODS	MEATS	FROZEN FOODS
BREADS	CEREALS	DAIRY	PET SUPPLIES
DELI ITEMS	BEVERAGES & SNACKS	PAPER GOODS & CLEANING	HEALTH/BEAUTY CARDS & GIFTS

25 THINGS TO TEACH YOUR TEENAGERS BEFORE THEY LEAVE HOME

How to:
- write letters.

- open, maintain, and reconcile a checking account.

- understand the principle of interest on loans and credit cards.

- save money in various types of high-interest drawing accounts.

- be assertive without being aggressive.

- care for babies and small children.

- find phone numbers of important resources (city utilities, poison control, physician referral services, etc.).

- pay bills, avoid late charges, and keep a general ledger of their accounts.

- sort laundry, use bleach, and read labels to give longer life to clothes.

- iron with various temperatures and starches.

- plan balanced meals and shop with coupons.

- use various kitchen appliances, timer ovens, and cookware.

- plan trips, use travel agents, and get through airports.

- schedule time for projects and commitments.

- find help if they get locked out of their car or house.

- buy gas, get the oil changed, and maintain a car.

- buy insurance.

- set goals.

- stay on a personal growth and life-long learning plan.

- learn new hobbies through local educational resources.

- know good values in merchandise purchases.

- know when to schedule routine doctor appointments.

- develop safety precautions (storms, flooding, tornadoes, power-outages, fire, etc.).

- clean house.

- trust God.

PART TWO
A TIME TO RECEIVE

There is also a time
when a mother must refresh herself
in the company of friends.
It is there,
through the love received from
others,
that she is built up
and made strong
to enjoy the days to come.

"If You Can Find a Truly Good Wife, She Is Worth More Than Precious Gems!"

Her husband can trust her, and she will richly satisfy his needs. She will not hinder him, but help him all her life. She finds wool and flax and busily spins it. She buys imported foods, brought by ship from distant ports. She gets up before dawn to prepare breakfast for her household, and plans the day's work for her servant girls. She goes out to inspect a field, and buys it; with her own hands she plants a vineyard. She is energetic, a hard worker, and watches for bargains. She works far into the night!

She sews for the poor, and generously helps those in need. She has no fear of winter for her household, for she has made warm clothes for all of them. She also upholsters with finest tapestry; her own clothing is beautifully made—a purple gown of pure linen. Her husband is well known, for he sits in the council chamber with the other civic leaders. She makes belted linen garments to sell to the merchants.

She is a woman of strength and dignity, and has no fear of old age. When she speaks, her words are wise, and kindness is the

rule for everything she says. She watches carefully all that goes on throughout her household, and is never lazy. Her children stand and bless her; so does her husband. He praises her with these words: "There are many fine women in the world, but you are the best of them all!"

Charm can be deceptive and beauty doesn't last, but a woman who fears and reverences God shall be greatly praised. Praise her for the many fine things she does. These good deeds of hers shall bring her honor and recognition from people of importance.

Proverbs 31:10-31

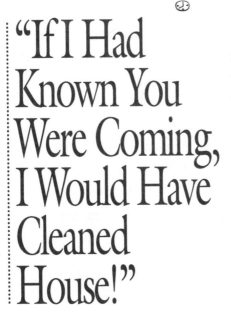

"If I Had Known You Were Coming, I Would Have Cleaned House!"

Even when Lindsey's mother worked outside the home, her house was always clean. Lindsey struggles with housework, but she happily reports that her children will also remember having a clean, clutter-free house. It was on a Friday—in September of 1992. She had cleaned house all day because her in-laws, who lived out-of-state, were coming to visit.

When their guests finally arrived, Lindsey's daughter ran to greet them shouting, "Grandma, Grandpa, hurry! Come see my room! It's picked up!" Lindsey hoped they would think she only had trouble keeping that one room straight. But after dinner her innocent daughter revealed the truth of Lindsey's facade when she cried out from the bathroom with a frightened voice, "Mommy, come quick! The toilet water is blue!" The little girl was even more bewildered by the sudden burst of laughter from her mother and visiting grandparents.

Was it worth taking a day off, without pay, to clean house for her guests? Was it worth making a special effort to impress her guests with blue toilet-bowl cleaner? Yes, the memory of how a clean house both surprised and frightened Lindsey's daughter has lasted much longer than the dollars she would have earned that day. It also gave grace for future visits when her job had progressed and she had deadlines that could not wait a day for cleaning house. The dust and scattered toys didn't matter so much the next time her in-laws came to visit, because they too remember the Friday that her house was clutter-free.

Guilt Buster

Spotless houses can produce ulcers if you push too hard for perfection.

 **Love Booster**

Show first-time visitors a clean house, but be sure to show them your heart also.

 Time Saver

Motivate your children to help clean house by making it a family affair. Play vigorous music and clean together room by room so you can visit as you work. Celebrate when the task is done.

 **Life Builder**

Lord, help me recognize the moments in the day that are worth remembering.

"All a man's ways seem innocent to him, but motives are weighed by the Lord. Commit to the Lord whatever you do, and your plans will succeed."

Proverbs 16:2-3

Spontaneous Entertaining

The traffic snarl gave Nancy time to mentally list her overdue household responsibilities. All the dirty clothes hampers were spilling over, and it was bill-paying time. Behind the steering wheel her tension eased as she realized she had a peaceful Friday evening ahead to catch up on virtually everything.

At home her husband grabbed a box of crackers and reminded her of a big sports event on TV. All the more reason for Nancy to swing into action. The next hour was a whirlwind of sorting clothes, backpacks, mail, and two-way inquisitions with children about homework assignments and chores. Fortunately, no one asked about dinner.

An unexpected knock at the door brought the house into a sudden frenzy. Tripping over the laundry on the kitchen floor, Nancy grabbed the barking dog. Her husband gently pulled their toddler out of the way, leaving Nancy to answer the door while bending over to hold the dog.

"Hi! said Bill and Suzie.

"Hi," Nancy answered back feebly.

"Are you not ready for us?" Suzie ventured.

Nancy's brain took several passes through her long- and short-term memory, then suddenly recalled extending an invitation to her friends for dinner. As she groped for something to say, Bill's burst of laughter saved her. They tumbled through the door, stepping over piles of dirty clothes and toys, and the house was soon filled with laughter, shouts, squeals, and wagging tails.

Years later, with Nancy still behind on the laundry, her sister reminded her of the evening she committed the ultimate faux pas. Nancy had forgotten the story since her embarrassment was lost in a raucous visit that went better than anything she could have planned. "What did I do?" she asked her sister.

"You ordered pizza and Suzie helped you clear a place at the table to eat!"

"Well," Nancy reasoned out loud. "That's probably what I would have served them even if I'd remembered they were coming."

Since no one is perfect, no one expects *you* to be. An unexpected visitor can be even better than being caught up on laundry!

 Make the most of entertaining opportunities with good humor and a little resourcefulness.

 Keep a list of food delivery numbers near the telephone!

 Lord, help me to prepare a table in the presence of my unexpected guests.

"Do not forget to entertain strangers, for by so doing some people have entertained angels without knowing it."

Hebrews 13:2

Honk If You Need Encourage- ment!

Erin walked into her office, threw her briefcase on the desk and said loudly, "This is it, I'm tired." Colleagues gathered in her doorway and smiled sympathetically as she told them horror stories of homework projects, car pool difficulties, and baby-sitter dilemmas that contributed to her state of exhaustion.

The people in Erin's office often made such "mood announcements" due to a general agreement between them to warn others when one was tired and irritable. Erin's down time always seemed to hit in September after her children were back in school and challenged with late night homework. In one short week, Erin could transform from positive and charming to positively alarming.

Katie, a manager in a subordinate position to Erin's, pushed through the doorway and took a seat across from Erin. "Remember the geese," she said with a smile, pointing at the picture on the wall in Erin's office.

Erin and Katie kept Canadian geese pictures in their offices as a reminder of teamwork, because the geese take turns being the

114

leader. The goose at the front of the v-formation has the most tiring flight since he faces the wind directly. The geese that follow have an easier flight because an uplift is formed by the flapping of wings from the geese in front. When the birds fly together they achieve at least seventy-one percent greater distance than if they fly alone. The lead goose is quiet, but those who follow honk to encourage those up front to keep their speed. When the leader tires, he drops to the back and floats on the currents created by the other members of the team. The geese know that taking turns means survival for all of them.

"I know something else about geese," Katie continued. "When a Canadian goose is wounded or ill, it drops out of the formation and lands to rest. Then two other birds drop out of formation and stay with the wounded member. When the wounded goose is able, they launch out to catch up with their group."

Erin smiled and thanked Katie for reminding her of their feathered examples of team players. She knew Katie was offering a helping hand with the work, and an understanding ear for her troubles. Just her colleague's smile and the reminder of the geese lifted her spirit.

It's okay to pass responsibilities to your teammates so that everyone has the energy (and the interest) to stay in the game.

 Renew your co-workers' strength by mentioning things you appreciate about them. Even better—tell their bosses when you see them do well.

 Keep a list of answered prayers or achievements to review when you or a co-worker needs a pick-me-up.

 *Lord, teach me to share both the load and the lead.*

"Though one may be overpowered, two can defend themselves. A cord of three strands is not quickly broken."

Ecclesiastes 4:12

Tilted Thinking

Ashley had a friend who always griped that it was easier for men to have jobs than women. "Listen," she told soft-spoken Ashley one Friday at lunch. "Compare the twenty minutes it takes for men to get ready in the morning to our minimum forty-five minutes. Men don't worry about their make-up, fingernail polish, accessories, or which purse to take. And often men work faster, but only because they give their work to someone else to do!"

Ashley answered by sliding a book she had been reading toward her, *The Superwoman Syndrome* (Warner Books). "Take this for the weekend," Ashley offered.

Monday, Ashley's friend said she was shocked to read about the gender-free tasks which men easily let others do. Men don't feel guilty about buying store-bought cookies for their children's class parties. Men hire housekeepers and let their secretaries respond to business calls. They enjoy meals prepared by caterers or restaurants and even let others shop for gifts.

Ashley's friend was the type who cleaned her house before the housekeeper came, and insisted she had to do all the shopping and make all the calls at work herself. She sheepishly admitted her fault in placing a sense of importance on routine tasks.

"What else do you know that I don't?" she asked Ashley.

"How about the *Time* magazine article a few years ago explaining the biological reason that male and female thinking patterns are different," Ashley said softly. "Six weeks after conception, the male baby's connection between the right and left hemisphere of the brain is severed by the male hormone, causing men to think primarily with the logical, left brain. Females process information on both sides of the brain, and tend to find decision making a slower process."

Both women sighed. "I guess I need to use my creative right brain abilities on important tasks, not the urgent or routine," the friend said.

"Or just tilt your head to the left when you have too much to think about," Ashley answered with a grin.

Guilt Buster Even the celebrated woman in chapter 31 of Proverbs delegated work to people who served her.

 Love Booster Say thank you to your husband or a male co-worker who offers advice that rescues you from unnecessary job tasks. And be willing to help him with creative alternatives when he needs ideas.

 Time Saver Evaluate whether a task will give temporary gratification or have an eternal impact. Then decide how much time you want to invest in the project.

 Life Builder *Lord, help me to work with love and a sound mind.*

"Therefore encourage one another and build each other up, just as in fact you are doing. Now we ask you, [sisters], to respect those who work hard among you, who are over you in the Lord and who admonish you."

1 Thessalonians 5:11-12 (author's paraphrase)

Managing Raul

Jamie sat stunned. "Raul is being moved to my department? But he hates women!"

"And he's arrogant too, but he's still our most competent foreman," the director answered sternly. "We need your project completed—under budget."

Jamie knew that once the bottom line was brought up, that was the end of the discussion. She started praying even before she left the plant. Stories of Raul had amused executives behind closed doors for twenty years, but they also kept Raul from promotions. The disappointment had embittered him toward all managers. By contrast, Jamie's record was flawless. Her high levels of productivity had repeatedly earned her accolades and promotions.

That weekend, Jamie listened to a teaching tape on how to lead men. Much of it was basic information to a woman who had bucked the corporate world for eleven years, until the speaker said, "A man will do anything for someone who will take a bullet for him." The wisdom was conventional in men's circles, but for Jamie it was revelation. After praying all weekend, when Raul reported to her office, Jamie told him what she had heard about him, both positive and negative.

"Raul, I'm convinced you are the person we need, even though your work history is tainted."

Raul shifted in his chair.

"However, I'm not like any manager you've ever had." Jamie continued, "If you fail, then I fail. I won't say my department came up short because of you. I'll take the fall. And I expect you to do the same. If you've got crewmen who aren't working out, I give you full authority to replace them. Just say the word and I'll go to personnel."

When Raul's mouth fell slightly open, Jamie knew she had penetrated his crusty exterior. She finished the meeting, stood up, shook his hand and said she looked forward to working with him.

In their next meeting, Jamie found much to praise Raul for. "I knew you were the one for this job," she said.

"Thank you for your confidence," Raul said, breaking into a little smile. "I think I'll be able to work for you."

Guilt Buster We can act like women when we work with men and still win their confidence and alliance.

 Love Booster Everyone responds to love and respect—the grocery clerk, co-workers, and our children.

 **Time Saver** Before filling precious hours with worry and anxiety, pray over *every* care and give God an opportunity to bring solutions.

 Life Builder *Show me ways to encourage others to rise to greater heights, while heading there myself.*

"The fear of the Lord teaches a man wisdom, and humility comes before honor."

Proverbs 15:33

When All Else Fails

Ashley did not consider herself a brave person. She dreaded having to face her boss to ask for more time off. She had already been put on probation for missing a week of work when her child had the chicken pox. Now her other child was sick, but her supervisor told her it didn't matter, she had to be at work today "or else."

Her husband agreed to stay home if Ashley appealed to her supervisor in person. Her husband was self-employed, and staying home from work jeopardized their livelihood. The fear of confrontation paralyzed Ashley, but her courage grew as she drove to work. The supervisor had spoken harshly over the phone, threatening "severe action" if she stayed out longer. Appealing to reason and sympathy hadn't helped Ashley's case.

She pushed the front doors open and squared her shoulders as she walked in the building. When she reached her hall, she glanced in the manager's door and noticed she was in her office. Ashley hesitated, her mind wavering in indecision.

The manager was her supervisor's boss. Should she go over her supervisor's head? Ashley's thoughts flashed to her child, then to how much money her husband was losing while staying home, so she quickly entered the manager's office. Ashley explained her situation as thoroughly and quickly as possible. She had rehearsed it well.

"Go home," was all the manager said.

Ashley didn't wait for an explanation. She rose, thanked the manager, walked out the door, and hurried to her car. Ashley thought perhaps her boldness caused the woman to violate company policy by hearing her, instead of referring her to the supervisor. A week later, Ashley timidly came back to work, not knowing what to expect. But no one, including her supervisor, ever mentioned her absence.

Guilt Buster When you can't change anything, charging forward may be your best and only choice.

 Love Booster Love means moving past our comfort zone for the sake of the ones we love.

 **Time Saver** Prevention always takes less time than a cure. Protect your family's health with flu shots, vitamins, and loads of fresh fruits and vegetables.

 **Life Builder** *Lord, keep my family free from disease and safe from harm today, in Jesus name, I pray.*

"The wicked flee when no man pursueth:
but the righteous are bold as a lion."

Proverbs 28:1 KJV

Woman's Best Friend

"Jessica is complaining of a sore throat." The school nurse's words hit Nancy like a sledge hammer. Nancy had just taken four sick days; two to care for her youngest daughter's strep throat and two to get over it herself. Now her oldest was sick.

"I'll call you right back," she told the nurse, and quickly called her husband at work.

"I'm still tied up with this project," he said. "Can your friend Linda pick her up?"

Nancy fought panic and frustration. She misdialed her friend's number the first time but finally connected.

"Hello." Linda's voice gave Nancy a rush of relief.

"Linda, I'm so glad you're there. Jessica's sick and I can't take any more time off. Are you free? Could you pick her up from school just for today?" Linda agreed. Nancy gulped some aspirin as she called the nurse, then leaned back in her chair and sighed, feeling fortunate she had a good friend like Linda.

When she picked up Jessica at Linda's that night, a black, furry puppy was snuggled in her daughter's arms as she lay on the couch. "Who's your new friend?" Nancy asked.

"Alex is his name, and Linda said I could keep him."

"What?" Nancy said, looking up at Linda.

"Can she keep her?" Linda asked sheepishly. "I should have only gotten one puppy, but I couldn't resist them both. Now I'm having second thoughts."

"So this is the pay-back for picking up Jessica? I have to keep the dog?" Nancy said laughing.

Nancy looked at the puppy licking Jessica's fevered face.

"We'll take him," Nancy said.

During the next few weeks the black, wiggly puppy gave Nancy's daughters hours of squealing fun and finally endeared itself even to her. Apart from digging in the back yard, Alex grew into a good dog and Nancy was happy she had agreed to take him. She just wished she could have changed his name to something that meant friendship, because that little wiggly body always reminded her of the day a friend came through.

Guilt Buster When you just can't be there for your family, it's okay to look for someone who can.

 Love Booster Puppies and other pets add more cleaning and responsibility to a home, but they also add life and laughter.

 Time Saver Use your days off carefully to allow time with your children when they can most enjoy you. If it's allowed, take vacation time around the holidays to extend your total time off.

 Life Builder *Help me find and cultivate true friendships with people I can count on.*

"*A* man that hath friends must shew himself friendly:
and there is a friend that sticketh closer than a brother."

Proverbs 18:24 KJV

Equal Pay

The baby-sitter called Lindsey at work to say she couldn't meet the children after school. Lindsey was frantically trying to leave the office when her husband, Seth, called to say hello. She explained that she had to leave early and that the project she was working on was taking more time than she had anticipated. She also had to prepare for a meeting the next day. He listened to her concerns and said, "I wish I could go home early today."

It was a beautiful, sunny day and Seth was already planning to mow the lawn when he got home from work. Lindsey sensed that he found her predicament enviable. Whenever someone had to miss work to attend to the children, Lindsey had naturally assumed the responsibility. They had never discussed it, but it seemed to be a given that Seth was the one who had to work and Lindsey's income was "extra."

They both silently considered the irony. He wanted to go home and she wanted to work—but tradition says the papa goes to work and the mama goes home. After years of hard work, Lindsey's contribution to their household budget was nearly equal to Seth's. They both had similar responsibilities that affected other colleagues if they were gone.

Silently the husband-wife team reached the same conclusion—the choice of who should go home was no longer automatic. Seth broke the silence first. "I'll go home and be with the kids. It's slow here today and I can get an earlier start on the things I want to do at home." More surprising than his unexpected offer was the fact that Lindsey didn't feel guilty about letting him go. In that spontaneous instant, the equality of their jobs gave each of them the freedom to work and to parent their children.

Guilt Buster

When you know the affairs of your household are in order, you can enjoy the work of your hands.

Love Booster

Help your family obtain their goals too, even when you are busy pursuing other projects.

Time Saver

Call a family meeting to discuss schedules for the coming week. Eliminate stress by asking about field trips that will need sack lunches, homework assignments requiring special supplies, recitals, or sporting events that will need transportation, and plan ahead for these family events.

Life Builder

Lord, give me wisdom to see that the work of my hands is profitable and the needs of my family are at the top of my "to do" list.

"She is clothed with strength and dignity;

she can laugh at the days to come."

Proverbs 31:25

Thyme For Dinner?

"I don't have time for this!" Shelly muttered. In an hour she was to meet two friends for coffee and a movie—a rare treat. But small accidents kept slowing her down. First it was the thyme. She fumbled in the cupboard for the salt and sent an open container of the herb careening out. Thyme leaves decorated the stick of butter below.

"Look Mom, there's something gross all over the butter!" Her child's objection made her decide not to leave clean-up until later. Her eyes traveled to the stove clock as she cleaned the mess. Fifty-five minutes remained to prepare dinner, eat, and change her clothes.

After she placed beef patties in a skillet, Shelly washed her hands, and stooped under the sink for a towel. Reaching for the towel, her hand bumped the bottle of window cleaner, which fell out of the cabinet spilling blue liquid all over the floor. In a previous rush, she hadn't tightened the lid after refilling the bottle and now she had to act quickly to keep the cleaner from lifting the wax from her kitchen floor. She fumed silently as she soaked up the fluid and carried the drenched, dripping towels to the laundry room.

By the time she returned to the kitchen, the cooking hamburgers smelled like they were just past the point of flipping. *Not again! The kids won't eat these if they're burned*, she thought glumly as she scraped the browned meat as best as she could. *I know! I'll make a picnic for them.*

She pulled out a checkered tablecloth and arranged bottles of condiments on it. A wicker basket of potato chips served as a festive centerpiece. Shelly smiled. She called the children as she set out burgers on paper plates.

"A picnic!" her youngest shouted gleefully as the others ran in. "These are delicious!" one exclaimed as they started eating. The others nodded enthusiastically.

Shelly's baby-sitter arrived and Shelly showed her where to dispose of the after-dinner mess, then happily set off for her evening out. As she pulled onto the street, she smiled to herself. Her efforts to do something unusual for herself had turned the supper hour into something unusual and exciting for her family.

Though you may fumble and stumble to make "thyme" for yourself, you can do it without cheating your family.

 Variety at the supper table is as important as salt and pepper.

 Keep plastic utensils in your silverware drawer so they are handy for children who might be tempted to take good forks and spoons outdoors. Replenish your supply of paper products regularly for emergency meals.

 Help me remember everyone benefits when I allow time for myself.

"You prepare a table before me....Surely goodness and love will follow me all the days of my life, and I will dwell in the house of the Lord forever."

Psalm 23:5-6

The Friendship Call

For several summers in a row, Lindsey's friend Emily had organized a weekly picnic for children from their church. When possible, Lindsey arranged for her day off to coincide. She liked being with Emily, and cherished the memories of watching her children laugh and play in the city parks and amusement centers.

Each time the children were to return to the bus, Emily beckoned them with a bird-like call. She cupped her hands to her mouth and bellowed, "Caw, Ca-a-aw!" Lindsey enjoyed watching the children obediently jump out of swings and scramble down from jungle gyms to return to their leader and proceed to their next destination.

Emily kept the group together all day with her unique call and made the children feel like they belonged to someone. Even Lindsey liked being part of the group who responded to the call. She wanted to do the call herself, but pride kept her from even trying.

When the church organized a weekend women's retreat, Lindsey and Emily decided to attend the camp together. Lindsey had to

work late, so Emily went to the campground ahead of her and promised to save Lindsey a bunk.

After getting the family settled and heading into the night alone, Lindsey felt left out and stressed as she drove to the retreat center. It was dark when she pulled into the campground and women were already going to and from various buildings. She had obviously missed the orientation and wasn't sure which building to go to first.

Just turn around and go back, she thought helplessly. Instead, she forced herself and her flagging spirits to get out of the car. Then she heard Emily's unmistakable voice, "Caw, Ca-a-aw." Turning in the call's direction, Lindsey spotted Emily standing in the light from a far-off building, waving at her. Lindsey quickly responded. "Caw, Ca-a-aw," she yelled ridiculously, then she laughed. Emily's call chased away all Lindsey's anxieties and loneliness. Once again, Lindsey felt like she belonged.

Taking the time to call a friend is the foundation of building life-long relationships.

 Never let pride keep you from telling a friend how much they mean to you.

 Find a way to whistle or call for your loved ones that is recognizable in a crowd or from a distance. If you can't whistle, beckon them with a call that they will recognize as your call to come home.

 Lord, call to me often so I will know the sound of Your voice.

Jesus said, "I am the good shepherd, and know my sheep, and am known of mine....And they shall hear my voice."

John 10:14,16 KJV

Seize the Day!

"It was good talking with you. Good-bye," Nancy said to her client and returned the telephone receiver to its cradle. She stared wistfully at the phone for a moment. She remembered when late afternoon phone calls at work were as often from one of her daughters as from a business client. When she wasn't there, her assistant would take the call and she would receive messages like, "We're out of milk," or "What's for dinner?" Now her girls were grown and living out of town.

Seldom did the mailbox produce news about her oldest daughter's career capers. And even fewer were the midday phone calls from her youngest inquiring, "Mom, what should I do about...?" Nancy was uncomfortable with the emptiness.

Hey, come on! Nancy told herself. *The last time they were this quiet, it was because everything was going well for them. Isn't this the way it's supposed to be?*

Driving home through rush-hour traffic, Nancy's mind wandered again down lonely trails. *I'm lonesome for their voices, and I yearn for a letter with its reassuring, "P.S. Mom, don't forget—I love you."*

Suddenly, she thought of her husband. *I should be pouring my attention and affection on him. I used to long for more time alone with him. Now that I'm not distracted with the children being here, I'm distracted with them being gone. They could be back any day with loads of grandkids. I'd better take advantage of today.*

Nancy whispered a resolution to focus on her husband and let the children lead their lives apart from her. With a renewed frame of mind, she pulled into her driveway and thought, *From now on I'm calling my driveway "Lover's Lane."*

After setting out candles for dinner Nancy checked to make sure there was popcorn for that evening, when she could cuddle up with her husband and channel surf for a good classic movie. Later, between handfuls of popcorn, she laid her head on her husband's shoulder and said sincerely, "I sure hope the kids don't call this evening."

Guilt Buster If there is a valid need, the kids will call!

 **Love Booster** Letting go of your children means fearing less and loving more.

 **Time Saver** Agree with your husband ahead of time on healthy limits to your involvement with your adult children.

 **Life Builder** *Lord, help me to adjust from the era past and not deprive myself of the era present.*

"I am my beloved's, and His desire is toward me."

Song of Solomon 7:10 NKJV

Who Is My Neighbor?

After stopping at the bank, Jamie headed toward home to do some last-minute preparations for a business trip the next day. Her finances were in a shambles since a car repair and a broken microwave had eaten up her last paycheck, and she felt fortunate to have forty dollars available to take on the trip. As she rounded the corner to get on the freeway, a woman carrying a baby stepped off the curb and flagged her over.

Jamie could have swerved to ignore the woman, but quickly surveyed the situation. A boy who looked about twelve sat nearby, apparently belonging to the stranded party. Armed with her cellular phone and her dog in the back, Jamie felt safe, so she pulled over to ask the woman what she needed.

The unfortunate mother had run out of gas miles away and hitchhiked this far to see if a friend who lived nearby could give her money for gas. As Jamie started toward the friend's house, choosing to spare her time rather than her money, her dog licked the boy's face and made an instant friend. As Jamie talked with the boy, a desire sprang up in her to set a good example for him and give him a memory he might keep for life.

Jamie struggled with herself. She was losing valuable time. But she knew what it felt like to be desperate. Only the year before she had run out of gas late at night, and once she had been stranded on the freeway with a flat tire and a car full of children. Her heart went out to the mother who so boldly flagged her down.

"I'll take you to get gas and then to your car," Jamie said, turning to get on the freeway, as she handed the woman her money. Jamie was instantly flooded with relief. She had filled a need in someone's life at her personal expense of time and money, and she had set an example for the boy in the backseat as he made friends with her dog.

Guilt Buster Everyone needs a good neighbor to help sometimes. When you need it, ask boldly and accept gratefully.

 Love Booster Dogs are not afraid to lick a face they like. If we will get over our inhibitions, we can become unafraid to spread our love around too, even to strangers in need.

 Time Saver When others are in a bind, do the right thing now instead of wasting time thinking about it. When you are in a bind, people may be more willing than you think to help provide for you and your children.

 Life Builder *Please give me all I will need to give to others today, Lord, and I will trust You to provide for me.*

"*Give, and it will be given to you. A good measure, pressed down, shaken together and running over, will be poured into your lap. For with the measure you use, it will be measured to you.*"

Luke 6:38

More Time-Saver Tips:

TICKLER FILE FOR FRIENDS AND FUNCTIONS

A box to hold 3 x 5 index cards with dividers marked January through December can become a helpful tickler file to remind you of seasonal functions and responsibilities. Make index cards for events that you need to remember during each month and file them behind that month's divider.

Title one card "Birthdays," and list all the birthdays of friends and family for whom you want to buy a card or gift. At the beginning of each month, simply pull the index card and take the list with you to the store to buy the cards you need that month.

Another index card might say something like, "Write to Christa and invite her and her family to visit during spring break.

More ideas for tickler cards to be filed in the appropriate month could include:

- Plan Mandy's birthday party (file in the month before her birthday).

- Fertilize the flower bed, lawn.

- Change the oil in the car.

- Get a perm (move it forward four months each time).

- Plant fall jonquil, tulip, hyacinth, and crocus bulbs.

A Time To Receive

- Write a Christmas letter and address holiday cards.

- Change the furnace filters (for maximum efficiency change them once a month, or buy permanent filters and wash them in the dishwasher once a month).

- Make hotel, rental car, plane, and ticket reservations for summer events and vacations.

- Go to Mayfest, Oktoberfest, Pecan Festival, etc. (list details on the card of when and where the festival will be. Also list phone numbers of places to stay or things to do when visiting that particular festival.)

The main idea is to make a card for anything you are likely to forget that is many months away, especially if it's repeated each year.

Adding A-Z dividers at the back completes the usefulness of this box by giving you a place to keep address cards for people you frequently call or to whom you write letters.

For more ideas on organizing your life with 3 x 5 index cards, read *Sidetracked Home Executives*, by Pam Young and Peggy Jones (Warner Books, New York, NY).

HOW TO DO TWO THINGS AT ONCE OR AT LEAST IN HALF THE TIME

We asked busy mothers to list ways they have saved or doubled their time. You may want to add these time-saving tools and techniques to your busy routine.

DOUBLE-TIME TECHNIQUES:

- While folding laundry, listen to a cassette about speed reading to improve your reading skills.
- Carry notecards in your purse so you can write to friends while waiting for children to finish lessons, or appointments.
- Find a dry cleaning service that will pick up and deliver to your office.
- Equip your car with a double-your-time supply kit: include a book to read, a nail file, clippers, polish remover, and clear polish.
- Whenever possible, schedule doctor, dentist, and haircut appointments for all your children at once.
- Do leg lifts and isometric exercises while washing dishes.
- Paint your nails before reading.
- Clean out a kitchen drawer or the refrigerator while waiting on something to boil or bake.
- Keep your junk mail and reading file handy to review while dialing phone numbers, waiting on someone to answer, or when you are put on hold.
- If you have highly coordinated motor skills, you can use the treadmill while reading a book and watching a documentary during the parts that interest you.

AS MONEY ALLOWS,

- Buy an answering machine. (Allows you to ignore interruptions when blocking time for yourself.)
- Order automatic call back, speed dial, call return, call block, and call waiting service from your telephone company.
- Get a gas credit card for a station that allows you to pay at the fuel pump.
- Install an automatic garage door opener.
- Purchase an automatic car door opener for your key ring.
- Sign up for automatic payroll deposit to checking and savings, and automatic bill paying deductions through your bank.
- Get a carry-all luggage bag (on wheels - it's not just for airports!)
- Buy an electric shoe-shine kit.
- Purchase a pager and a purse-sized cellular phone.
- Get a portable tape player to listen to books on tape or motivational seminars while doing housework.
- Install light sensors for your front porch light and indoor light timers. (This keeps you from having to pull back into the driveway, unlock the front door and turn the porch light off as you leave the house in the mornings.)
- Order season tickets to family parks and theaters (saves trips for cash and tickets).
- Use quick-dry nail polish spray.
- Use a high wattage (1600) hair dryer to speed up styling time.
- And hire a maid, a cook, and a housekeeper, of course!

EPHESIANS CHECKLIST FOR WIVES

Because this part of the book is about relationships, we wanted to include something about taking time for our spouses. Like anything else in life, what you put into a marriage determines what you will get out of it. Instead of waiting for your husband to make the first move to treat you like a queen, demonstrate your love for him by practicing godly attitudes toward him.

After commanding men to love their wives as themselves, Paul explains in the Bible the attitude wives are to have toward their husbands. *The Amplified Bible's* expanded translation offers a checklist for wives to consider in their responses to their husbands:

> *"However, let each man of you (without exception)*
> *love his wife as [being in a sense] his very own self;*
> *and let the wife see that she respects and reverences*
> *her husband—that she notices him, regards him,*
> *honors him, prefers him, venerates and esteems*
> *him; and that she defers to him, praises him, and*
> *loves and admires him exceedingly."*

Ephesians 5:33 AMP

A Time To Receive

Write down ways in which you may consciously esteem your husband as the Bible instructs wives to do. Then check them off as you successfully portray these attitudes towards your husband. Ask God for help if you find it difficult at first.

Respect _____

Reverence _____

Notice _____

Regard _____

Honor _____

Prefer_____

Venerate _____

Esteem_____

Defer to _____

Praise_____

Love _____

Admire_____

Remember, emotions follow actions.

SCRIPTURAL PRAYERS FOR YOUR FAMILY AND FRIENDS

The Bible is God's Word, written to you right where you are. You can insert a person's name where another name is, because God is not a respecter of persons and what He will do for one He will do for all. He is the same yesterday, today, and forever, so He will still do today whatever we have seen Him do in the past. His promises to others in His Word were not just for the heroes and heroines of Bible times, but are available to you right now.

James, the brother of Jesus, wrote in his letter to the Church that we do not have what we want because we don't ask God, or because we don't ask according to God's will. (See James 4:2-3.) But when we pray according to God's will, we are assured that we will receive the things we ask for. (See 1 John 5:14-15.)

Ask God to bless your spouse and children with the promises from His Word. *The Amplified Bible* gives greater explanation of what the original Greek and Hebrew words meant and will help you understand how God's promises apply to your everyday needs.

The prayers below are paraphrased directly from God's Word and illustrate how you can pray according to God's will for your family. Pray for your family every day, choosing verses with meaning. Then insert your loved one's name where it fits like this:

A Time To Receive

Psalm 1

Lord, bless _____ and give him wisdom to ignore the counsel of the wicked and to avoid the way of sinners and those who scoff at the things of God. Thank You for nurturing _____ so that he thinks of You day and night. Your love makes him to be like a tree planted by rivers of living water so that he will bring forth fruit without failing. Thank You for watching over him and causing him to prosper.

2 Thessalonians 3:5

Thank You, Lord for directing _____'s heart into realizing Your love and into the patience that comes from Christ.

1 Thessalonians 5:23

You are the God of peace Who sanctifies _____ totally so his whole spirit, soul, and body are preserved blameless unto the coming of our Lord Jesus Christ. Thank You for keeping _____ separated from profane things.

1 Chronicles 29:19

Lord, give to _____ a perfect heart to keep Your commandments, testimonies, and statutes and to do all that You have called him to accomplish.

Ephesians 1:17-18   God of our Lord Jesus Christ, the Father of glory, give _____ the spirit of wisdom and revelation in the intimate knowledge of You. I pray also that the eyes of _____'s understanding are enlightened, that he may know the hope to which You have called him and the riches of Your glorious inheritance You have given to him through Christ.

Ephesians 3:16   I pray, Lord, that out of Your glorious riches You will strengthen _____ with power in his inner man by Your Holy Spirit, so that Christ will dwell in his heart by faith. I pray that _____ is rooted and grounded in love so he may comprehend with all saints what is the breadth, length, depth, and height of Your love. May _____ really come to know through personal experience the love of Christ which passes knowledge so he might be filled with You.

Philippians 1:9-10 I pray that _____'s love towards others may abound so that he will learn to sense what is vital, and approve and prize what is excellent and of real value, recognizing the highest and the best, and distinguishing the moral differences. I pray that _____ remains untainted and pure, unerring, and blameless, so that with heart sincere and certain, he may approach the day of Christ's return not stumbling nor causing others to stumble.

Colossians 1:10 Lord, I pray that _____ may be filled with the full knowledge of Your will in understanding all spiritual wisdom and discernment in spiritual things. May _____ live in a manner worthy of You, Lord, fully desiring to please You, being fruitful in every good work, increasing in the knowledge of God, and strengthened with all might according to His glorious power to exercise all patience and longsuffering with joyfulness.

Colossians 4:12 I pray that _____ may stand perfect and complete in all the will of God.

Colossians 3:2 May _____ set his affections on things above, not on things on the earth.

- Remind your family how much God loves and cares for them, and that He has great plans to bless them as they follow His commands.

- When you speak to them or about them, confess what you know God is doing in their lives instead of dwelling on the problems they are having.

- Read Deuteronomy 28:1-14 to them, which reveals God's desire to prosper them, so they will understand what a loving God we have watching over us.

- Put your hope in God, for He can do far more than you can even ask or think.

> *"This is the confidence we have in approaching God: that if we ask anything according to his will, he hears us. And if we know that he hears us— whatever we ask—we know that we have what we asked of him."*

1 John 5:14-15

PART THREE
A TIME TO UNDERSTAND

*S*ometimes
we mistake facts
to be truth.
Truth is not found
in the explanation of
what happened,
but truth is found in understanding
why something happened.
Truth is found in the motives
and intentions of the heart.
We must look for truth
and not just facts
when we review the stories
of our lives.

Create In Me a New, Clean Heart, O God.

Create in me a new, clean heart, o God,
filled with clean thoughts and right desires.
Don't toss me aside, banished forever from your presence.
Don't take your Holy Spirit from me.
Restore to me again the joy of your salvation,
and make me willing to obey you.
Then I will teach your ways to [my children],
and they—guilty like me—will repent and return to you.
Don't sentence me to death. O my God, you alone
can rescue me.
Then I will sing of your forgiveness, for my lips
will be unsealed—
oh, how I will praise you.

Psalm 51:10-15 TLB (author's paraphrase)

Painted Nails

The line at the post office was excruciatingly slow. Looking at her watch confirmed Jamie's fears—in a few minutes she would be late getting back to work from her lunch hour. Holding the package pick-up slip crumpled from a week-long ride in her purse, Jamie determined not to turn back after making it this far.

A suntanned, muscular woman with a little boy was putting the clerk through postage aerobics at the counter. Jamie could see the woman was upset, but judged that it had to be about something less important than keeping her job. Priding herself in her ability to handle stress, Jamie thought, *I wish a silly postage problem was all I had to worry about.*

Already agitated by impatience, Jamie felt a prick of jealousy as she noticed the woman's well-shaped and polished fingernails which boasted, "I don't type or do dishes." She imagined that "Mrs. Fancy-free" probably had a husband who earned a sizable income, affording her the opportunity to stay home and enjoy her children while basking in the sun or working out. The woman's beautiful hands reminded Jamie that it had been days since she had polished her own nails.

A Time To Understand

The child dangling from the woman's arm caught Jamie's attention and smiled. Seeing her return the smile, the little boy waved, then grasped his mother's leg.

Taken in by his friendly grin, Jamie waved back to the little boy, forgetting for a moment that she was irritated with his mother for taking so long. Then she noticed that the little boy had been completely quiet through the entire transaction. Suddenly his mother turned to him and made a sign with her fingers.

As Jamie watched the mother and son walk away, she realized that the little boy was deaf. She couldn't help but gaze at how the boy lovingly watched his mother's beautifully groomed hands. As Jamie drove back to work with her package safely tucked by her side she was thankful that all she had to worry about was being late to work.

Guilt Buster Comparing yourself to others is a waste of time. Everyone deals with their own issues their own way and no one is without problems.

 Love Booster Shape and polish your nails right before your reading time.

 **Time Saver** Buy a can of quick-dry nail spray to speed up your home manicure.

 Life Builder *Lord, let the conversation of my mouth and the communication from my heart be beautiful in Your sight.*

"Happy is the man that findeth wisdom, and the man that getteth understanding. Length of days is in her right hand; and in her left hand riches and honour."

Proverbs 3:13,16 KJV

Straining At Gnats

Due to a burst of corporate growth, Erin's division's vice-president asked her to make way for new staff by moving to a smaller office, which meant giving up a large executive desk for a much smaller one. Believing that the size of her desk made a statement about her value, Erin was hurt by the request to move. After all, she had played a big part in spurring the growth. Then she remembered the advice of a friend who told her to ask God for the truth whenever her feelings were hurt. "The truth will set you free!" her friend had explained.

Erin took her anger, hurt, and bruised self-image to God in prayer and asked if it were true that she was esteemed lowly by her colleagues. Instead of a flow of reassuring affirmations to bandage her wound, the most surprising thought came to her. *I don't even like the desk I'm giving up.* The desk was big, contemporary, and masculine with a dull rubbed finish that didn't reflect the warmth and character of her personal style. How foolish to demand the right to a desk she never liked! She was straining at the gnats of appearances, while swallowing a camel of bitterness.

The new office was cozy, convenient and much more comfortable than the cold, stark room Erin had left behind. Its quiet location gave her solitude and enabled her to accomplish more work in less time. She was glad she had not confronted her boss. When she went straight to God with her injury, He cut a new groove to help her out of an old rut.

Erin has learned to avoid hurt feelings by looking for the truth *before* she takes offense. If someone says her report isn't clear, she asks how it can be improved. If someone doesn't like her idea, she looks for other places to use the concept. If her husband doesn't want to go camping during the school holiday, she searches her heart and sometimes discovers that she really prefers a more convenient holiday than the work camping requires. She is learning to enjoy walking in truth.

Recognize your leadership capability by the number of people who want to be like you, not by the number of people who want your desk.

 Being a team player wins you more than the game. God has good things planned for those who humble themselves and trust Him.

 When troubled, ask God to reveal the truth in the story. Looking for the truth in a situation sets us free from impending heartache.

 Lord, keep me from straining at a gnat when I could be enjoying Your mercy.

Jesus said, "But you have neglected the more important matters of the law—justice, mercy and faithfulness. You should have practiced the latter, without neglecting the former. You blind guides! You strain out a gnat but swallow a camel."

Matthew 23:23-24

Hidden Extras

Shelly's co-worker returned from lunch waving cruise tickets. "In two months Sam and I will be swimming the shores of the blue Caribbean!" Those nearby smiled at her excitement.

Shelly concealed her jealousy with rejoicing and an animated suggestion. "That's a good excuse for a new wardrobe!" As usual, the display or mention of life's "extras" pushed Shelly into the doldrums of self-pity.

Earlier that morning, another colleague arrived brandishing a new ring. "I didn't really need it," she explained, "but my husband lets me do what I want with my check." *My check. His check.* The words played in Shelly's mind. *Do you know what it's like to provide the only check?*

At coffee break the conversation turned to home computers. Their supervisor announced she couldn't wait to check the mailbox at home. The CD ROM encyclopedia she ordered would arrive this week. It cost only $79.00.

Since Shelly's divorce, she had worked full time just to provide family necessities. Surplus was rarely available. Her children were well-fed, adequately clothed, and comfortably housed, but there was no room for "extras."

That evening Shelly faced her discontent alone. *Mom's solution for everything was "make a list,"* she thought. *Maybe if I list the less tangible blessings in my life, I can find something to rejoice over.* The counting began. She didn't work nights. She was never asked to work overtime. The woman who watched her children after school was nearby and the best surrogate mother she could ask for. Her work benefits now included retirement, insurance, and sick leave. Her children had good teachers at school. She belonged to a great church. She loved her mother and father.

Fifteen minutes later, Shelly had a list of many hidden "extras" in her life that she knew others would give anything for. Regardless of what she lacked, the blessings she had were more than enough to give thanks for.

Guilt Buster

No child who has his mother's love and acceptance is poor.

 Love Booster

Think often of the benefits God gives you each day. Let an attitude of appreciation burn inside you that warms your family and shines a light to those around you.

 Time Saver

Save time and earn money. Ask friends if you can bring your resalables to their garage sales. As a gratuity, pay them a percentage of your profits.

 Life Builder

Lord, help me recognize my assets and not bemoan my liabilities.

"Blessed be the Lord, who daily loadeth us with benefits, even the God of our salvation."

Psalm 68:19 KJV

The Bribe

Lindsey thought it would be wonderful when she landed a job that allowed her to travel. Leaving her normal routine always expanded her viewpoint and inspired her creativity. On one of her business trips she had an opportunity for a day of sightseeing, but her conscience struggled for permission to enjoy the extra benefit.

Both excited by the possibility and exhausted by the conflict of "abandoning" her family for four days, Lindsey decided to ask her children if there was something she could do or buy for them so they would grant her their blessing for the trip.

Her negotiations began, "Girls, I have to go on a business trip again, but I want to make it up to you. What can I do to show you that I really love you, even though I have to be away for awhile?" Wise enough to recognize the opportunity that had just been given to them, the girls looked at each other to search for clues before they committed. Suddenly her ten-year-old daughter's face brightened as her own negotiation skills came alive within her. Lindsey felt nervous about the price tag her daughter was about to put on her penance for absence.

"How 'bout you buy us some fruit roll-ups?" her daughter suggested.

"Yeah!" the other two cheerfully agreed.

"That's it?" Lindsey asked, not knowing whether to be relieved or offended. "You will happily be rid of me for a $1.89 box of fruit roll-ups?"

Her daughter's expression was suddenly serious again. "Oh no, mother," she quickly responded. "We each want our own box!"

 Children don't always miss us as much as we miss them.

 Praise your children when they manage to handle new responsibilities without your supervision.

 Talk to your children when you feel you have neglected them. Children are great problem-solvers and often have an instinct for what it takes to pull the family together.

 Lord, help me to know the difference between the times the children truly need me and the times I am needing them.

"Do not fret or have any anxiety about anything, but in every circumstance and in everything by prayer and petition [definite requests] with thanksgiving continue to make your wants known to God."

Philippians 4:6 AMP

Make History

Jamie almost skipped to her front door, she felt so full of life. Against what she thought was her better judgment, she had signed up for a night course at a large university. She dashed home from work that first night, quickly stirred a casserole together, changed clothes, then served it up with steaming vegetables as she said good-bye to her husband and sons.

"But what are *we* going to do?" her youngest asked.

"You're going to clean the kitchen, take baths, and go to bed on time—but without me," she answered, hoping they would actually do it.

Jamie kissed him and left for three glorious hours on her own. She flew past the routine stops of a mother's life—doctor's offices, soccer fields, and malls—and headed into the heart of the big nearby city that she barely knew. The adventure of driving there was reason enough to forget her concerns for her family. She listened raptly to a fascinating lecture, then talked with interesting classmates without being interrupted.

The wonderful evening had brought a new sense of life to her, but she was instantly deflated as she walked into the living room of her home. In front of the television sat the children and her husband. She scanned the kitchen. It was clean, but it was past their bedtime. Her peace was shattered by anger that without her they couldn't follow the simplest routine.

"Mom, look!" her youngest said. "The Berlin Wall is coming down."

Jamie's rage instantly stopped and she scooted in between her sons to watch the historic event of people receiving their freedom. After thirty minutes, she marshaled the children to bed and fell asleep herself, completely exhausted and elated. It was a night never to be forgotten by Germany—or by Jamie.

Three years later Jamie drove the stretch of road heading for the university with her oldest son. A little thrill tickled her stomach. "This is where I used to go to my class," she said pointing to the university.

"Remember the night we stayed up late to watch the Berlin Wall coming down?" he asked.

"That *was* a memorable evening," she said smiling.

Guilt Buster The world doesn't stop when we take time for ourselves, and it may even improve.

 Love Booster Our families must grow beyond dependence on us.

 Time Saver Learning to make simple meals can be just as nutritious for the family as it is emotionally nutritious for you.

 Life Builder *Help me to enjoy the freedom You have given us to grow and pursue our goals.*

*J*esus said, *"I am come that they might have life, and that they might have it more abundantly."*

John 10:10 KJV

"We Don't Do This"

Nancy was exhausted. It had been a very long day. Everyone at work was waiting on her for something. She sat in her minivan for a few minutes before tackling the bags of groceries in the back. *Just get through dinner,* she thought with a grimace.

As she started the evening meal, children traipsed through the kitchen with homework questions, complaints of siblings removing certain items from their rooms, queries about when were they going to eat, and an introduction to a friend who was staying for dinner.

Many times Nancy wanted to shoo everyone away, order pizza, and leave for the movies. Instead, the dinner came together. She hurried to set out the steamed vegetables and popped a tray of biscuits into the oven. "Okay, let's pray," she yelled, a hint for two wayward family members to come to the table.

The family said "Amen" just in time for Nancy to take hot biscuits out of the oven.

"Mmm," her oldest daughter said. "Those look good."

"Sure do," her visiting girlfriend blurted out. The girl blushed since this was her first visit and everyone looked at her.

"So, what did everyone do at school today?" Nancy's husband asked. "How's swimming?"

The question brought excited conversation from a table full of kids who competed on local swim teams. Nancy's youngest son was especially animated with a female guest at the table and ended the meal by entertaining the giggling girls with funny faces.

"Come on," Nancy interrupted, "let's clear the table and get the kitchen cleaned."

The children moved slowly into action but were soon bumping and chattering in the kitchen. Administrating from the sink, Nancy finally had a chance to talk to her daughter's guest. "Is your house this busy?" Nancy asked.

"No," the girl answered, looking down. "I mean, we don't do this."

"Do what?" Nancy asked.

"We don't eat dinner like this, except on Thanksgiving."

Nancy paused. The girl's statement relaxed her and she reflected on her earlier mood. *At least I'm doing something right,* she thought. As Nancy drove the girl home later, she invited her to come for dinner any time.

Guilt Buster When mining, there is always more dirt than diamonds. Sometimes just pressing on is the most you can do, and often it's all that is needed.

 Love Booster Give your family what you can—a meal, a gift, or the benefit of your education—with love.

 Time Saver Technology, such as frozen foods and dishwashers, continues to shorten meal preparation, but shared responsibilities have stood the test of time as the number one asset to a mother's work.

 Life Builder *Lord, thank You for letting me know the times I really am doing the right thing.*

Love "always protects, always trusts, always hopes, always perseveres."

1 Corinthians 13:7

Happy Meals are for Kids

By the time Lindsey arrives home from work, her husband and two oldest daughters have already been home for an hour. As she walks in the door, their eyes turn away from after-school TV programs and their voices sing in unison, "What's for dinner, Mom?" She usually frowns and tells them she will think about it while she is changing clothes. This gives her time to work on the resentment she feels towards the little vultures who seem to only want her home so they can eat.

Two things amaze Lindsey about this routine. One, that after all these years as a working mom, she still doesn't consistently plan a menu for her family. Two, that after all these years of proving that she never knows what is for dinner, no one else takes the initiative to start dinner without asking her.

Returning to the living room, she asks them what they want to eat. Immediately her future homemakers shout the names of restaurants instead of food groups. Seeing that Lindsey is not moving towards the refrigerator, her husband smiles and picks up his wallet and car keys.

Once at the restaurant, their youngest daughter shouts, "Let's go to the playground!" and happily leads her big sisters outside while Seth and Lindsey order their children's favorite foods.

The cashier smiles at Lindsey as he hands the tray of food to them and thanks them for coming to their restaurant.

Lindsey smiles back and silently gives thanks for people who are still working to prepare their evening meal, even though she has already been off work for an hour.

Guilt Buster

We may not always create a perfect meal, but a happy mood still makes the meal memorable. Salad bars are still a nutritious option when eating out.

Love Booster

A joyful heart makes a melody that's contagious and helps the digestive system too.

Time Saver

Use the meal-planning system on pages 56-60 and post the menu on the refrigerator. Teenagers who are first to arrive home can begin parts of the meal that require extra time. Add instructions to the menu that explains when to put casseroles in the oven or when to start potatoes.

Life Builder

Lord, thank You for the table you prepare before my family and me—even at fast food restaurants!

"Sing and make music in your heart to the Lord, always giving thanks to God the Father for everything, in the name of our Lord Jesus Christ."

Ephesians 5:19-20

❧

Inconveniences

Ashley attempted to take the folded sheets to the linen closet upstairs, but her son's big dog, her daughter's small dog, and the family cat, all fell in line in front of her, behind her and between her legs as she climbed the stairs. Once the sheets were tucked away, the parade trotted back in the same fashion. When she sat to read the mail, the canines flopped on the floor and the cat parked on the neighboring chair.

Just like the kids, she thought, remembering when her teenagers were youngsters who followed her around the house. That was when she first realized the facts: People are inconvenient. No matter where she went, a parade of two-footed creatures followed her, along with their squabbles and questions. The children now had busy schedules, so their four-footed counterparts were trying their hardest to stand in for them.

When Ashley's mother retired and moved to be near her family, she learned the corollary to the inconvenience rule: *More* people are *more* inconvenient. With every added relationship, inconveniences mounted. The kids got sick the night before important meetings. Her mother had urgent needs in tandem with the trouble at work. Colleagues took trips when they were greatly needed.

Ashley surveyed these creatures that had become surrogate inconveniences. She remembered times her children had given her reason to enjoy the better moments of life, such as catching tadpoles and butterflies while exploring nature trails. Many nights her mother brought delicious meals to them, knowing Ashley was exhausted from over-commitment at work. Colleagues carried her load when she had to be away. Ashley sighed.

The big dog raised his head to see if she was moving. In one short year, his owner would be in college and the dog would remain with her. Ashley smiled at his attention to her every move, and he wagged his tail in reply. She could never feel the same for him as for his master, but she was glad to have these loving reminders of the inconveniences in her life. She tried to get up quietly, but one by one they all rose to follow her again.

Guilt Buster

No one is wild about their parental role every moment of every day, nor does every mother feel the emotion of love when told that a book which is necessary for a homework assignment is still at school. Yet love overlooks the inconveniences of life.

Love Booster

Look for opportunities to help someone you love with something that is troubling them.

Time Saver

Save yourself some legwork when picking up the house. Carry a basket in which to put things that belong in other rooms. Leave one room of the house for another only after you have replaced the items from the basket that belong there and have collected everything that needs to go to another room.

Life Builder

Lord, thank You for not seeing me as an inconvenience, but as someone for whom You would lay down Your life.

"For God so loved the world, that he gave his only begotten Son, that whosoever believeth in him should not perish, but have everlasting life. For God sent not his Son into the world to condemn the world; but that the world through him might be saved."

John 3:16-17 KJV

"Mom, I Want...

It was a drizzly, wet Sunday afternoon and all of Shelly's kids were at friends' houses but one. The ten-year-old boy's boredom had turned to misery. "No wonder I'm bored," he complained to his mother. "We're so poor. We don't even have a video game or computer. If you were married, at least we'd have some money."

As his voice droned on, Shelly looked at the whiskered faces in the newspaper article she was reading on the homeless.

"Everyone has more money than we do," he muttered. "Maybe you could get a different job. Or maybe you could get another one besides—"

"Get in the car," Shelly said softly.

He obeyed, assuming that his mother had finally given in and he was in for a trip to the store. But when the city skyscrapers came into view, the boy realized he wasn't going all the way downtown just to buy a new toy. Shelly drove slowly past the men and women slouched in doorways, sprawled on sidewalks, drinking and playing cards on park benches. Past the food line that snaked around the corner and up two blocks. Past hungry women and children, never saying a word.

When she came to the cardboard village under the freeway overpass, she allowed her son to get out and give a little boy on the curb the fifty cents he had in his pocket. They were headed home before he finally broke.

"Mom, I can feel it," he said, straining to keep his tears back.

"What?"

"My heart breaking." He started crying.

Once the emotion subsided, Shelly and her son could hardly stop talking about the sights, sounds, and smells of the places they went, nor could they rid their eyes of the faces of needy, hungry people in their own city. He eagerly told his siblings about it when they came home, and they all joined him in nagging Shelly again.

"Mom, can we please forget Thanskgiving this year and help feed people on the streets? PLEASE?"

You cannot carry all your children's pain for them. It's okay to allow them to experience some of the gritty realities of life.

 Instead of trying to give your kids what you didn't have, make sure you give them what you do have.

 You will save more than just time when you realize you can often show more love by saying no than by saying yes.

 *Lord, help me not to jump in to rescue my kids when they are feeling the pain of life that will mold their character and make them grow in Your plans and purposes for their lives.*

"For each one should carry his own load."

Galatians 6:5

I Surrender

Repeatedly Ashley thought, *If I was a stay-at-home Mom, I would be in better control of everything. I'd control the popsicles so they wouldn't get eaten so fast. I'd monitor the applesauce so we could have it on the night I served pork chops, and I'd eliminate the emergencies that could have been scheduled before becoming emergency status.*

Ashley sat, chin in hands, at the kitchen table, far from the worries of work, sipping a cup of tea, and contemplating what could be. Home–that place where she controlled her universe. Byron suddenly burst through the back door with wide eyes and blurted out, "Mom, I almost got hit by a car!"

"What?" she gasped. "Where?"

"Just across the street! Right there, Mom!" He pointed toward the front yard.

She followed him outside and listened to his complicated explanation. She clutched him and whispered, "Thank You, Lord." She tensed as she considered again what had almost happened and squeezed Byron tightly. "Be more careful, son," she said seriously as she released her grip.

She slowly walked inside and sat down. *I should have been watching him,* she thought at first. But she had to dismiss the guilt because she realized she simply couldn't watch every child every minute. Then the words she had thought a hundred times came to her, that if she were at home all the time everything would be great.

What made me think being home could cure everything? she thought. *I can't control storms or lightning, the airways over international airports, or the school bus driver, so what made me think I could insure the safety of my children?*

Ashley whispered another prayer. This time she surrendered to the season of life she was in and put her trust in the plans God had for her and her family.

Guilt Buster

To think we can control the outcome of everything is great egotism; to attempt to control everything is even greater folly.

 Love Booster

True faith operates every day, whether we realize it or not, and allows us to love others by letting them out of our control.

 Time Saver

Worry is a substitute for prayer. Every time you are tempted to waste time in worry, stop and pray, which will strengthen your trust in God.

 **Life Builder**

Lord, remind me to ask for the courage and strength You offer when I must face unfortunate circumstances; and send Your angels to protect my family today.

"And let the peace of God rule in your hearts...

and be ye thankful."

Colossians 3:15 KJV

Shadows Are More Fierce Than Reality

Shelly's insurance company wasn't going to pay! Her son had allergies so severe, their family doctor had referred them to a special allergy clinic. According to the clerk at the insurance company, that clinic was not covered.

By the time Shelly arrived home that night, her mind had raced past every current concern and had focused on her son's future—a life crippled by inactivity and severe restrictions due to life-threatening allergy attacks. She considered every alternative, including quitting her job and going on public assistance, which she remembered covered allergy testing.

She snapped at the children when she arrived home, remained tense, and awoke during the night to walk the floors and worry. Finally, she prayed and went to sleep. The next morning, she called the insurance company armed with her best arguments.

"Oh, that's covered," the clerk said when Shelly stated why she called. "We must have misunderstood you yesterday."

Shelly was relieved, then angry with herself for fretting so much the night before. Now she faced a day without proper rest, she had been angry with her children, and there was no crisis after all. It had been a simple misunderstanding. She quietly laughed as she remembered she had learned this lesson once before.

When she was ten, she had had to walk home in the dark after a birthday party. She had heard a noise behind her, so she stopped and turned around. But it stopped too. She walked faster and heard it again, so she ran all the way home with her heart pounding in her throat. As she walked through her front door, she noticed that the jump rope she had been given as a party favor was hanging from her pocket, its wooden handle was bumping along the ground and trailing her all the way.

"Shadows are more fierce than reality," her father told her that night. She resolved never to spend another minute in fear or anxiety without fully researching all the facts.

Guilt Buster

Shadows cause many people to run, but those who face their fears are rewarded with laughter when the light reveals the empty threats of darkness.

 Love Booster

Take all your cares to God and allow Him to show He cares for you.

 Time Saver

Before accepting the fear and worry that cuts you off from others, check the facts. When the instructions or policies of a store or company are unclear, call the company several hours or even minutes later to get another opinion from a different clerk or representative.

 Life Builder

I will trust in You, Lord, and not lean on my own understanding.

"For the weapons of our warfare are not carnal, but mighty through God to the pulling down of strong holds; Casting down imaginations, and every high thing that exalteth itself against the knowledge of God, and bringing into captivity every thought to the obedience of Christ."

2 Corinthians 10:4-5 KJV

The Schoolhouse Door

When her daughter started pre-school, Lindsey walked to the school room and made sure she felt welcomed and settled. Eventually, Lindsey participated in the student drop-off plan. Parents drove their cars to the front of the building, where an intern teacher opened the car door and escorted the children through the gate, across the playground, and into the big doors for school.

One morning her family overslept and Lindsey had an important meeting for which she had to be on time. When she pulled up to the school gate, the playground was empty and the intern was already inside. To park the car and walk her daughter to the door would have added another ten minutes to her tardiness. She asked her daughter if she could manage the gate and school door by herself.

"No problem, Mom," the little girl answered. Like a big kid, she picked up her backpack and lunch box, opened and closed the car door, then successfully maneuvered the latch on the fence gate. As she approached the schoolhouse door, Lindsey watched her shift her backpack and lunch box to her left hand to open it with her right. Suddenly she looked so small and the school door looked so big. After a brief struggle she got both bags and body inside where Lindsey knew her teachers would greet her and take over.

A painful lump formed in Lindsey's throat. How could any meeting be more important than walking her child the fifty feet to the door? What did this ten minutes really gain for her? She cried on the way to work, not completely understanding why she was so upset by the picture of her daughter walking through the school door alone.

Looking back years later at the still-disturbing memory, Lindsey saw that her grief wasn't about her guilt for not walking her daughter to the door. Her sadness was caused by the bittersweet anguish of watching her child take steps toward independence. Her little girl was big enough to go through the gate and open the door all by herself. It was a feat to celebrate, not one to regret.

Guilt Buster — Giving our children opportunities to do basic things on their own builds their confidence and self-esteem.

 Love Booster — Praise your child for small things that are done correctly.

 Time Saver — Keep your children's shoes in the coat closet or in a basket by the front door so you will always know where to look for them when you are in a hurry.

 Life Builder — *Lord, when I am feeling guilty about things I should be celebrating, help me see what I am missing.*

"And ye shall know the truth, and the truth shall make you free."

John 8:32 KJV

More Time-Saver Tips:

CALENDAR OF EVENTS AND GOALS

Managing your time multiplies your opportunity to enjoy your family and friends while still achieving goals and fulfilling commitments. Keeping a daily planning system can save you hours each week by organizing information and objectives in a method that is easy to retrieve. There are many business planning systems and calendar books, but we list Daytimer, Inc., in Allentown, Pennsylvania, as the example of a daily planner that can bring order to the many events you must administrate as a working mother. Or, you can begin with a small notebook to keep with you at all times to record the following information:

- Place a month-at-a-glance calendar at the front the notebook. Record events that are out of the ordinary on the monthly calendar. Significant meetings, seminars, parties, or anything that requires a major block of time that day should be recorded here so that you don't double-book.

- A week-at-a-glance calendar like the example following this list, enables you to block off large amounts of uninterrupted time to work on time-consuming projects. When you are able to see that a period of two or three hours will be your only opportunity to work on something for the whole week, it is easier to say no to other invitations that would distract you from your goal.

- Remember to block off time to plan and a time to pamper yourself during the week. It may work to block off different evenings to do laundry, clean, buy groceries, write letters, entertain guests, and schedule a "family only" night.

- Next, keep a master list of things to do as they are assigned to you in chronological order at the front of your notebook.

- Finally, your planning system needs a day-at-a-glance page so you can schedule hourly appointments.

- Choose six tasks to list at the top of your page and plan for blocks of time in your day to work on creative projects. You may want to list four work-related and two personal tasks for your daily goals.

- Keep phone numbers of frequently called friends, work associates, and teachers in this planning system. Bus schedules, insurance numbers, calling card numbers, gift basket shops, and service numbers are good to keep with you at all times.

HOW TO KNOW WHAT TO DO FIRST

- List five projects that are competing for your attention. Then use the following steps to determine which task is the most important, rather than the most urgent task to work on first.

- Compare the importance of #1 to #2 and put a check mark by the one that is the most important. Then compare #1 to #3, again putting a check mark beside the most important of the two, then compare #1 to #4, and so on.

- Next compare #2 with #3 checking the more valuable project, then compare #2 with #4, and #2 with #5, always putting a check mark by the project that has the greatest payoff if completed.

- Compare #3 with #4, and then #3 with #5, checking the one that is greater of the two.

- Finally, compare #4 with #5, then count the total number of check marks beside each task.

- Place a "1" beside the job with the highest number of check marks, a "2" beside the one with the next highest, and so on, thus numbering them in order according to priority.

Task Listed Here:	Comparison checked	Order of Priority
Unpack boxes from move	✓	#4
Write the Rush Hour book	✓ ✓ ✓ ✓	#1
Hang dining room drape		#5
Bake pies for Thanksgiving	✓ ✓ ✓	#2
Plant Fall flowers	✓ ✓	#3

Often, it is still difficult to decide priorities, because as you can see, writing this book could be put off for at least a few hours while baking pies for Thanksgiving dinner. So compare priorities by deciding which task has the highest recognizable impact on others at work (or home) in the immediate future.

Or, ask yourself which task has the highest impact from a brief to moderate investment of time.

Work on the three projects that received the highest number of check marks from these comparisons and enjoy an immediate sense of success.

Use the weekly planner on the next page to reserve blocks of time for these important tasks.

SEIZE THE DAY

"To play, to rest, to think, to jest, to work to do your best" "Seize the day—Today"

Weekly Planner for the week of _____

TIME	SUN	MON	TUES	WED	THURS	FRI	SAT
8:00 am							
8:30							
9:00							
9:30							
10:00							
10:30							
11:00							
11:30							
12:00pm							
12:30							
1:00							
1:30							
2:00							
2:30							
3:00							
3:30							
4:00							
4:30							
5:00							
6:00							
7:00							
8:00							
9:00							

#1 Goal of the Week: _____

Steps to Objective	Starting Date:	Completion Date:

Obstacles to Achieving Goal	Solution:

Actual Results: _____

*"So be careful how you act; these are difficult days. Don't be fools; be wise: make the most of every opportunity you have for doing good. Don't act thoughtlessly, but try to find out and do whatever the Lord wants you to. Don't drink too much wine, for many evils lie along that path; be filled instead with the Holy Spirit, and controlled by him." (*Ephesians 5:15-17 TLB)

PART FOUR
A TIME TO BELIEVE

A woman must first believe
in the need for balance
in order to protect the time it
takes to obtain it.
She must first refill her own supply
of purpose, vision, and hope
before she can nuture
others.

There Is a Right Time For Everything

A time to be born; a time to die;
A time to plant; a time to harvest;
A time to kill; a time to heal;
A time to destroy; a time to rebuild;
A time to cry; a time to laugh;
A time to grieve; a time to dance;
A time for scattering stones; a time for gathering stones;
A time to hug; a time not to hug;
A time to find; a time to lose;
A time for keeping; a time for throwing away;
A time to tear; a time to repair;
A time to be quiet; a time to speak up;
A time for loving; a time for hating;
A time for war; a time for peace.

Ecclesiastes 3:1-8 TLB

NO MORE BAKE SALES

Ashley's husband took their children canoeing for the weekend and left her with two and a half days to enjoy doing whatever she wanted. A friend who had never seen her city was visiting from out of town and the timing seemed perfect. All that stood between Ashley and total freedom was an obligation to cook for the church bake sale.

Friday night Ashley ran to the grocery store for chocolate chip cookie ingredients. When she returned, her friend's voice on the answering machine beckoned for a late dinner and night out. Ashley was thrilled. What a change of pace!

Saturday morning she slept in, more from necessity than luxury, and woke up with the cookies nagging her. She slipped on her robe and stirred up a double recipe of cookie dough before it was time to show her friend the familiar sights in town. In the afternoon, her friend refreshed herself while Ashley made tray after tray of cookies and cleaned the house during the eight-minute intervals between batches.

When Ashley returned from another night out, she still had more cookies to bake. Standing in the kitchen late that night, dropping cookies onto a sheet, she battled exhaustion by reminding herself what a great, noble thing she was doing, pitching in with all the other mothers.

The next morning she rose early to drive her friend to the airport. Then she raced home, packaged the delicious morsels into bags with bows, struggled into a skirt and heels, and set out for church. There she watched as her little bags, twelve in all, were sold for just 50 cents each. She stood to the side, feet aching, head pounding, her weekend of fun escaping her, realizing what she had given up for just $6.

Her pastor's wife approached smiling, and Ashley told her what she had contributed.

"Working mothers shouldn't cook for bake sales," the wise woman said.

How obvious, Ashley thought. She couldn't have her weekend back, but it was worth the pain to be relieved for life from the duty of bake sales.

 **Guilt Buster**

You could donate the cost of cookie ingredients directly into the fund-raiser account!

 Love Booster

Saying no to unessential duties allows you to say yes to friends and family.

 **Time Saver**

When setting your priorities, remember: Doing what you truly enjoy speeds by in a flash, but doing what you are not suited to makes time drag.

 Life Builder

Lord, help me to try less but do more, and make every effort to do what leads to peace and builds up others.

"For the kingdom of God is not meat and drink; but righteousness, and peace, and joy in the Holy Ghost."

Romans 14:17 KJV

Briefcase Homework

Every evening, Lindsey thought she needed to bring work home to be ready for the next day at the office. Knowing the assignment was impossible to attend to until after the children went to bed, she hurried through the dinner each night, then nagged her children to do their homework and grumbled about how long it took them. Most nights she sent her children to their rooms with an angry reprimand. It was a pitiful routine.

Lindsey seldom even opened her briefcase before falling into her own bed, exhausted and frustrated over another unproductive evening. Something needed to change, but her kids had shown no interest in that "something" being them.

Lindsey finally decided to leave her briefcase and her work at the office. The difference was immediate. The first night she didn't feel rushed through dinner. By the third evening Lindsey discussed homework with the children while she folded laundry. At bedtime she tucked the covers around each child and then crawled in beside her youngest daughter to hear her prayers. The little girl snuggled against her mother, wrapping her arms around Lindsey's neck. She was so close that Lindsey could feel her daughter's chest rise and fall as her heart began to fill with dreams. The smell of her daughter's hair was sweet and the softness of the girl's cheek against her own stunned her.

"Mommy, I love you," the girl whispered. She fell asleep without an argument.

Lindsey hadn't worked on reports when she brought her briefcase home, and she wasn't working on them now. Yet she had found a secret to be better prepared for tomorrow. Tomorrow her children would remember the embrace of their mother's arms around their insecurities and would face their day with confidence. Tomorrow Lindsey would arrive at work rested and refreshed, and would smile over yesterday.

Just about any job task can wait until tomorrow, but your children are only this age once.

 Hugs and kisses before bedtime set the stage for sweet dreams. Even a mother hen is wise enough to cover her chicks while they are small, knowing they will soon outgrow the need for her protection.

 Tuck your children into bed at night instead of sending them off to their room. It is surprising how much a child is willing to tell you if it means staying awake a few more minutes. It is at the bedside that stories are told and mysteries unfold.

 Let me feel Your arms around me, Lord, and fill me with the joy of Your presence.

"I will take refuge in the shadow of your wings until the disaster has passed."

Psalm 57:1

When Enough Is Enough

It was election time at the Chevy Club and Josh was again nominated as the Social Chairman.

"You're not going to accept it, are you?" Erin asked as they drove the familiar route to the meeting.

"No, I guess two years has been enough," her husband answered.

"I'll say," Erin said emphatically. "We've attended every single club meeting and function, even when the kids had other things scheduled. I'd like to have the option to pass sometimes."

"Come on. It hasn't been that bad."

"Josh, do you realize we bought the new camper in June and it's now September, but we still haven't had a weekend free to take the kids camping?"

"Okay, okay," Josh said, "I said I'm not accepting it."

That night Josh was greeted enthusiastically as usual. He was the good-ole-boy who never met a stranger and whose hand every man wanted to shake. He sat in front with the officers as the elections began.

When Josh was nominated, Erin smiled confidently. But suddenly, the election was underway, Josh was unanimously elected, and Erin's ears were burning with fury.

"I can't believe it," was all she trusted herself to say on the way home. She silently asked God to reveal the truth about this situation.

When her emotions cooled, they talked. "Do you really want to do this?" Erin asked Josh.

"Not really," Josh shrugged. "I guess I just got caught because no one else wants the position."

"Perhaps that's because they know how much work it is, and they all have families too."

Josh drafted a resignation letter and put it in the club newsletter. At the next meeting, Josh recommended the club fill the position with a committee of three men, so no one was overburdened. His proposal was unanimously accepted.

"Why didn't I do that last year?" he asked Erin on the way home.

"Because you're such a nice guy," she said smiling. Erin admired her husband. "But thank you for doing it now."

 **Guilt Buster** It's okay to cry "uncle" when activities reach their limit. Just do it with respect and love.

 Love Booster Instead of keeping the kids busy, try a stay-at-home night once a week and play games with them.

 Time Saver Relax and reflect on difficulties until a simple solution comes to mind. Sometimes the only way to gain more time is to cancel something.

 Life Builder *I'll go where You want me to go, Lord. Help me to know the difference of when to say no and when to say "yes."*

*"Trust in the Lord with all thine heart;
and lean not unto thine own understanding. In all thy
ways acknowledge him, and he shall
direct thy paths."*

Proverbs 3:5-6 KJV

Have Grandma Do It

As usual, Nancy felt guilty about not doing more—especially spending more time with her kids. But it was Saturday, her only full day off, and regardless of what the family did, someone had to clean. As she bustled around, her eight-year-old daughter decided to make the family's lunch.

Nancy was in the family room, just beyond the breakfast bar, when her husband walked into the kitchen. Surveying the jelly on the kitchen counter and gooey, lopsided sandwiches on a serving tray, he burst into laughter and pinched his daughter's cheek.

"Honey, you better have Grandma teach you to cook."

Nancy's head shot up and she glared at her husband. The statement tipped over a bucket of worries, guilt, fear, and anxieties inside her. All she heard were haunting accusations:

"Mommy hasn't taught you very well."

"Mommy never cooks for us anymore."

"Mommy isn't a good cook."

"Mommy doesn't spend enough time at home."

"We'll see about that," she said hotly, and stormed into the kitchen.

That night, still somewhat mystified at her reaction, Nancy's husband apologized for his comment. The entire family knew his mother was the best cook in town, so his remark was a logical suggestion. But Nancy had become a whirlwind that afternoon, baking a cake with the girls, cleaning the house, and barking orders to let him know she was unhappy.

When he apologized in the quietness of their bedroom, Nancy burst into tears and told him the volumes of condemnation his innocent comment said about her. They talked it over and he assured her she was more than competent. Then he suggested Nancy lower her standards or get outside help.

"You could always have *your* mother teach the kids to cook," he said with a mischievous smile. This time Nancy laughed with him.

"Have Grandma do it," became a punch line that always broke tension and got a laugh in Nancy's family. And it became her husband's secret code to let her know she didn't need to be a superwoman to be a successful wife and mom.

 **Guilt Buster** Admit you are only one person and let others help you accomplish your goals.

 Love Booster When you are on edge, forget about "things" and "activities" for the moment and concentrate on being good to the people around you.

 Time Saver If you have a Monday through Friday work week, try cleaning house on Thursday night. The principle is that work fills the time available. By limiting yourself to one evening, you will have less distractions and more motivation to finish. This way you will be free to enjoy a more relaxing weekend.

 Life Builder *Please make me hear the needs of others louder than I hear my own worries.*

"Humble yourselves, therefore, under God's mighty hand, that he may lift you up in due time. Cast all your anxiety on him because he cares for you."

1 Peter 5:6-7

Cash Crunch

As soon as Jamie put cash in her purse, it seemed like it was gone. She doled it out for lunches. She sent it to a football game. It left to spend the night with a friend. She used it for tickets to the skating party. She sent it to school for the field trip. She needed it to buy something for an art project. The pizza man got it at least once a week. And if her husband raced out of the house in a hurry, he took it all. But whenever Jamie needed money, it was nowhere to be found.

She scrounged through her purse at afternoon breaks, looking for quarters to buy a soft drink. She sat at toll booths and rummaged through the ashtray to find the exact change. When she was short a few cents in the cashier's line at the grocery store, she smiled through embarrassment as people behind her handed over their coins. She even saved small expense reports to cash in so she could buy a regular lunch every now and then.

One day, after giving away every penny to family members as they filed out the door, Jamie decided to make a change. She went to the bank and withdrew twenty dollars, which she placed in a special part of her wallet to be her own private stash.

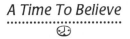
The first morning of her secret liberty, Jamie stopped on the way to work and bought a café latté, then sat in the parking lot and savored every sip. But by the next day, her private stash had found its way into every pocket except her own. And although she clung to the idea in principle, in practice having her own cash became a rare and cherished delight.

As Jamie approached the coffee stand each morning, she would check her purse. On some mornings, to her amazement, she would pull out enough money to savor some time alone with a delicious latté.

 **Guilt Buster** It's okay to indulge in something you enjoy sometimes.

 Love Booster When we give money we have purposely set aside for others, we show provision. When we give money we have saved for ourselves, we show sacrificial love.

 Time Saver Put a set amount of money in an envelope each payday. Keep it in a safe place, and seal it when you see it begin to dwindle.

 Life Builder *Thank You for providing for my family and me, and for giving us the desires of our hearts.*

"But thou shalt remember the Lord thy God: for it is he that giveth thee power to get wealth, that he may establish his covenant which he sware unto thy fathers, as it is this day."

Deuteronomy 8:18 KJV

Gilt Gift

Ashley listened to her husband's last-minute instructions. "Remember, I gave Hannah her medicine this morning, but she'll need it tomorrow morning. And Byron's Cub Scout party is at 12 tomorrow. Can you manage?"

"Yes," Ashley answered, forcing a smile.

"Are you sure you'll be okay while I'm at the retreat?" he asked.

Ashley nodded, hiding her weariness. At ages two, four, and six, the children overwhelmed Ashley so often that her husband had voluntarily taken over the chauffeuring and everything medical, including staying home from work when one was sick. Ashley felt her husband deserved this men's retreat more than any other man, and she was determined to send him off without a worry.

"We'll be fine," she said hugging him. "Don't be silly."

That night Ashley's confidence crumbled when the baby's dinner fell to the floor, Ben flooded the bathroom playing war games in the tub, and Hannah coated herself with Ashley's makeup. The next day was no better, trying to get everyone ready to shuttle Ben to his party and back. Nevertheless, Ashley persevered, and her husband came home that night to a clean house and children.

"Oh, Hannah's medicine!" Ashley exclaimed as he walked in the door.

"She'll be all right," he said, sweeping his wife into a hug and placing a small gift in her hands. As he reached for the children, Ashley opened the wrapping to find a tiny book about mothering with beautiful gilt-edged pages. Ashley drew a warm bath while her husband read a bedtime story to the children. As she soaked and read her little book, tears spilled down her cheeks. In no way did she resemble the writer, who reveled in marvelous motherhood. Her husband found Ashley soaking wet and sobbing, and gently helped her to bed.

That week Ashley placed the beautiful book on an end table as a decoration. She determined never to read it again, but cherished her husband's gilt gift. Although she couldn't effortlessly manage a household, she had mastered love. The little book resonated with beauty and meaning even when she felt her life didn't.

Guilt Buster We may not be like the women in the gilt-paged books, but our families value us more than gold.

 **Love Booster** Loving our children starts with loving their father.

 **Time Saver** Invest time getting to know other mothers who can share time-saving tips and even chauffeuring duty when you need help.

 Life Builder *Lord, help me to do the best I can and trust You with the rest.*

"The gift of God is eternal life through Jesus Christ our Lord."

Romans 6:23 KJV

Off Duty

The telephone rang. "Can I borrow two eggs?" It was Karen, the nurse next door. She had worked the swing shift for ten years.

"Home during the evening, Karen? You haven't quit, have you?" Nancy asked.

"No, I'm off-duty for the next three days."

"Off-duty!" What soft-sounding words. That's what Nancy wanted. A slip of time now and then to be "off-duty." *Would it be that hard?* Nancy wondered.

Her neighbor came and picked up the eggs, then Nancy prepared for bed, the hands on her wristwatch pointing to nine-fifteen. She put away the last T-shirt from the laundry basket, applied "age-defying" face cream, and threw back the bedspread. She knew that if she didn't retire by nine-thirty, lack of sleep would take its toll on her body the next day.

"Mom," came a call from the other room, "how can I write this sentence in the active voice?" Nancy's teenagers did not always fit her schedule. Sport practices often delayed their homework, and their youthful bodies seemed to oppose the need for sleep.

As she slid into her slippers and walked down the hall, Nancy remembered her life before she went back to work. There were solitary mornings when she returned to bed after the kids got off to school, and quiet afternoons before they arrived home when she enjoyed mini-retreats. Those memories seemed like a fantasy now that she had to leave the house at seven in order to be at work on time. In half-hope and half-desperation she prayed, "Lord, You have solutions for everything. How can I arrange some evenings by myself?"

When she finally returned to bed, her husband joined her. She told him an idea that was forming. "Why don't we take turns being off-duty sometimes," she said. "Of course, one of us would always have to be on-duty, but the other could enjoy uninterrupted time alone."

He agreed, and the next night they put the plan into practice–Nancy first. It worked! Nancy heard her children in the hallways and kitchen, but they respected the "off-duty" sign she tacked to the door. She painted her toenails and read a book while they dried, then started a list of things she would accomplish on her next "off-duty" night.

 Children need to know that Mom doesn't quit, but sometimes she is just "off-duty."

 Even family vacations are sometimes no vacation for Mom. Carve out times with your family when you are truly relaxed so they can see you as the fun person you really are.

 Place messages on "stickies" in key places around the house. A posted note will maintain the flow of inter-family communication when Mom is "on-duty" again.

 Lord, give me a peace that dispels the unrelenting lie that I am indispensable.

"Because of the Lord's great love we are not consumed, for his compassions never fail. They are new every morning; great is your faithfulness."

Lamentations 3:22-23

Bring Your Own Refill Cup

The clock struck half past ten and Lindsey was still awake. She knew she should try to sleep but she wasn't tired, so she quietly slipped out of bed without waking Seth. *Finally, a moment alone,* Lindsey thought as she settled into her favorite reading chair. *I will only stay up for an hour,* she determined as she considered how she might use this unexpected gift of time.

She had been so busy lately, she hadn't had time to evaluate why she was doing certain things or what she would rather do if given the opportunity. Her thoughts rushed into this quiet moment with the full force of midday tensions. *Relax!* she told herself. *Be still.*

It was then she heard the simple symphony of her life again. The refrigerator motor was humming, a night bird was singing, and a distant train whistle pierced the neighborhood's silence, soothing her senses as she relaxed more deeply into her chair. The living room was picked up, and she could see the kitchen was clean. It occurred to her that in spite of a hectic schedule, parts of her life *were* getting easier.

A Time To Believe

Her daughters now ironed their own shirts and helped with the housework. The family finally kept the living room clear of shoes, school books, and other unnecessary clutter.

Lindsey recalled many things to be thankful for. Even the team at the office seemed to be getting along better, making daily tasks easier. *Some things just take time,* she concluded as she fondly reviewed the past fifteen years of being a working mother.

Picking up her journal and pencil from the table beside her chair, Lindsey listed changes she would still like to make in her life. She began, *#1—Simplify my life so that I will have more times like this to rediscover what truly brings me joy.* As she continued to write, she was amused by the sound the pencil made while scratching her goals into a visible plan. She wanted to remember the feeling that she had from this quiet time alone, so she wrote, *When I am quiet, I find that simple things give me great pleasure. I must be quiet more often.*

Guilt Buster

Taking time alone empowers you to deal with the demands of your family by allowing you to think of creative ways to handle their various needs. Time alone refills your cup with enthusiasm for life.

 Love Booster

Time alone can turn into time with God. Elijah looked for God in the wind, the earthquakes, and the fire, but found Him in a still small voice. Quiet times are essential to spiritual growth.

 Time Saver

When you can't sleep, use the time to talk to God. He will enjoy the time with you.

 Life Builder

Lord, thank You that I am never completely alone because You are always with me.

"*O Lord, you have examined
my heart and know everything about me.
You know when I sit or stand. When far away you
know my every thought. You chart the path ahead of
me, and tell me where to stop and rest. Every moment,
you know where I am. You know what I am going to say
before I even say it. You both precede and follow me, and
place your hand of blessing on my head. This is too
glorious, too wonderful to believe! I can never
be lost to your Spirit! I can never get away
from my God!*"

Psalm 139:1-7 TLB

Car Tunes

"I found a new '57 Chevy," Josh announced gleefully. Erin smiled at him.

"You'll sell the other one first, won't you?" she asked.

"If I can, but I can't pass up this one."

Erin tried to stay positive as she continued preparing dinner while four kids slowly made their way to the table from sports practices, friends' houses, and phone calls upstairs.

The Chevy Club was a huge part of Josh and Erin's lives. It had given the family many hours of enjoyment with memories of car rallies, races, and mini-vacations created from car club activities. Yet Erin had always felt the club was more Josh's hobby than hers. That night Erin bared her soul to him. "I can't see investing more money in another car," she started. "At some point, I'd like to have a hobby too."

"What?" Josh asked with amusement, as if Erin had just announced a desire to defeat world hunger.

"Well, I'd like to go to concerts with my girlfriends."

"So nights out with the girls is now a hobby?" he asked, still laughing. He sobered when she didn't join him. "So get tickets for the concert season, but thanks for not making me go with you." Josh leaned over and kissed her on the cheek and Erin finally laughed.

Erin and three friends bought season tickets to the concert series and spent six wonderful nights reveling in good music, friendship, and hours apart from children and cares. The next year, they renewed their season passes without a second thought.

Guilt Buster After your family's needs are covered, it's no sin to spend some money on yourself.

 Love Booster Let the dishes pile up for a day to make time for a hobby, and get the whole family involved if you can.

 Time Saver Strengthen your network of friends by spending time together. You will be happier, and it will build stability into the framework of your family's life.

 Life Builder *I want to give in when it's necessary, so Lord, please help me know when I need to sacrifice and when You've already done it for me.*

Jesus said, "Whatsoever ye shall ask the Father in my name, he will give it you. Hitherto have ye asked nothing in my name: ask, and ye shall receive, that your joy may be full."

John 16:23-24 KJV

Holy Rest

Shelly heard the hostile tone in her voice as she told her son to pick up his room. "I'm disgusted with the mess, I'm annoyed because you have neglected it, and I won't wait any longer."

She was tired—over-tired. Fatigue had produced her ugly attitude. The all-night firecrackers over the July 4th weekend and Monday night's "sorry wrong number" call at midnight had shoved her over an invisible edge and started her week off wrong. Her limp spirit and weak body soured life for everyone around her.

The time for a sanity-saving nap eluded Shelly and she trudged on. But by Tuesday night, as she listened to herself bark at her son, she decided to take drastic measures. Relying on friends and ingenuity, she forced herself to rest somewhere other than her comfortable bed at home. By the end of the week, she had taken refuge by slumbering half her lunch hour on the office lounge sofa, in the back seat of her car, and on the lawn at a nearby park. On Thursday, she even borrowed her neighbor's downstairs guest bed after cooking the children hot dogs and telling them they could watch TV for an hour.

By the end of the week, Shelly was refreshed and invigorated in body and spirit. The places she chose to rest had refreshed her

creativity of mind, and her body was the happy recipient of energy. Soon her home and job were in harmony once again and a peaceful weekend awaited her.

Guilt Buster Before you get down on yourself for being edgy, think back to the last time you really rested, then take care of it.

 Love Booster God created rest. Awaking from a nap, you will find everyone around you is easier to live with. "Sleep...knits up the ravell'd sleeve of care."– William Shakespeare.

 Time Saver Begin a cache of frozen dinners for the nights you retire from the kitchen to the bed. You can make your own nutritious heat-n-serve by freezing leftovers and labeling them with contents and date.

 Life Builder *Lord, help me to work hard, smile often, and forgive always, so that I will sleep easy.*

"In vain you rise early and stay up late, toiling for food to eat—for he grants sleep to those he loves."

Psalm 127:2

Step Beyond Excellence

Lindsey spent many sleepless nights wishing her hair was *always* perfect, her clothes immaculate, her attitude excellent, and her performance flawless. She pictured herself receiving awards for outstanding contributions to her home, office, and community. Lindsey also wished she could stop wanting recognition.

Lindsey did believe she could reach a higher level of achievement. Delving into books about goal-setting and organizational skills, she improved her work and study habits. She scheduled larger blocks of uninterrupted creative time to work on specific projects. The more she accomplished real goals, the less she worried about whether or not others noticed her contributions.

Eventually, Lindsey realized her "Superwoman Vision" had been a cover-up for her fear of rejection. She laughed at the thought that if she ever met such a too-good-to-be-true model of perfectionism, she probably wouldn't want to be like her. Finally, in studying the "virtuous woman" of Proverbs 31:10-31, Lindsey was delivered from the superwoman complex.

Lindsey discovered the virtuous woman was capable, intelligent, reliable, comforting, and encouraging. She was an eager worker who used the best materials. She shopped, planned, and delegated to others in her household. She was wise and profited by buying, investing, and selling. She gave to the poor. Her family was warm, secure, and well-clothed. Her husband was respected in his circles and she was his crowning joy. She was optimistic. She gave kind counsel and wise instruction. In spite of her busy work, she oversaw her household and was praised and loved by her family. Beside all that, she feared God.

The virtuous woman endeavors to have it all, similar to the aspirations of a superwoman. But where a superwoman is motivated by the desire to please others, a virtuous woman is inspired by the passion to please God. A superwoman depends on her own strength. A virtuous woman depends on God.

Once Lindsey understood the difference in motivation, going a step beyond excellence became a short hop instead of the wide gulf she had imagined. She simply needed to please God each day. The rest would naturally follow.

Don't try to be a superwoman. You would just lay guilt on all your friends if you successfully became one.

 Being a godly woman brings hope and encouragement to all those who want to follow your Christ-like example.

 Find pleasure in knowing God, and He will give you the desires of your heart. (See Psalm 37:4.)

 Lord, help me to be the kind of woman who is loved and appreciated for who I am, not for what I do.

"The fear of man bringeth a snare:
but whoso putteth his trust in the Lord shall be safe."

Proverbs 29:25 KJV

The Balancing Act

Working mothers seem to need permission to balance their responsibilities. Many authors offer help to cope with hectic demands on our lives. Ann Morrow Lindbergh spoke of a woman's need to be alone in her classic book, *A Gift from the Sea* (Pantheon Books, New York). Erin was nineteen when she first read that book. Twenty years later she looked for it again because, as a working mother of four, she remembered the book held wisdom for her.

Dr. James Dobson teaches in his family film series that women need time to be together to exchange stories and compare what is normal and what isn't. He points out that women are more isolated now than two generations ago. Women used to cook and wash together while their men worked in the fields, but now many women feel no one understands the load they carry. When Jamie heard this teaching she took more time to be with her friends and was strengthened by the accountability she had with other women who committed to pray together.

Finding a balance between work, worship, rest, and play was the emphasis of Richard Exley's book *The Rhythm of Life* (Honor Books, Tulsa). It was placed in Ashley's hands at a time when she needed to quit working at play, playing at work, worshipping at rest time, and resting at worship.

A Time To Believe

In his book, *The Three Boxes of Life* (Ten Speed Press, Berkley, CA), Richard Boles encourages readers to develop a life-long blend of learning, working, and playing, instead of entering and leaving the boxes of education, work, and retirement. Nancy continued her education after reading his book, and has since enjoyed promotions at the corporation for which she works. She is even pursuing her dream of a musical career on the side.

The many books by Alexandra Stoddard have played a significant role in Lindsey's life beginning with her title, *Living a Beautiful Life* (Random House, New York, NY). Lindsey now takes time to put flowers in vases and uses her Sunday dinner plates more often. By enjoying the beautiful things around her, Lindsey has developed a contagious enthusiasm for life.

Shelly gleaned valuable perspectives from Gloria Chisholm's book, *Huddle Up* (Fleming H. Revell, Grand Rapids, MI). She learned that families need to be cheerleaders for each other. Gloria explains that faith isn't about control, it's about giving control to God. As a busy single parent, Shelly felt she learned parenting objectives from Gloria that she could easily reach.

These and many other authors give us permission to enjoy life. We tell our children there are some things in life we must endure, and we can endure these things with happiness or unhappiness. We encourage them to choose happiness and pursue the balance that will bring peace to their lives.

God doesn't want you to work hard doing something great for Him. He wants you to enjoy His greatness.

 Enjoy the balance of God's grace and power in Your life.

 Read books that help you to seize the day.

 Lord, lead me beside still waters where my soul can be refreshed.

"A just weight and balance are the Lord's:

all the weights of the bag are his work."

Proverbs 16:11 KJV

More Time-Saver Tips:

TAKE TIME TO BE ALONE

Find time to be alone.

Time alone can become time with God.

Time with God can bring a revelation of Truth.

Truth empowers you with direction and sets you free.

To be free is to be rid of guilt and condemnation.

Guiltlessness infuses joy into your life.

Joy breeds enthusiasm.

Enthusiasm means to be "en theo" or "in God."

Enthusiasm is contagious.

Find time to be alone.

FOUR STEP RUSH HOUR REDEMPTION PLAN

When you are alone to think and plan, consider ways to 1.) simplify your life, 2.) clear away the clutter that distracts you from focusing, 3.) set goals, and 4.) remove obstacles that keep you from achieving your dream.

STEP ONE: Simplify your life!

List two or three ways you could presently simplify your life.

1. _____

2. _____

3. _____

What day can you plan your weekly goals? _____

What day of the week can you pamper yourself? _____

Reserve time on your planning calendar to plan and pamper yourself.

List people who need to be aware of your new "time alone" schedule.

1. _____

2. _____

3. _____

Explain to your family and friends that you must make effective use of your time. They will soon enjoy the benefits that result when you take the time to be alone to think and plan for happiness and peace of mind.

STEP TWO: Clear Away the Clutter.

Evaluate your home and schedule. Look for unnecessary activites which clutter your time. Eliminate as many steps as possible and bring simplicity to your life.

What area of your home is cluttered and confusing?_____

_____

What can you do to organize or clear it? _____

_____

When can you schedule a block of time to clear it away?

_____

Make the same analysis of your office and schedule.

_____

_____

_____

Reserve time on your planning calendar to organize areas in your home and office.

STEP THREE: Set Your Goals.

Set goals, assuming there is no limit on your dreams. You can list both short and long term plans.

How could you improve your health? _____

_____

With whom would you like to develop a better relationship? _____

_____

What would make you feel more effective at work? _____

_____

What would you like to do to enhance your personal growth? _____

_____

What changes would you like to make to your home? ____

_____

What would you improve or change about your lifestyle?

_____

What would you like to change concerning your financial situation? _____

_____

STEP FOUR: Remove Your Obstacles.

Evaluate what circumstances are keeping you from reaching your dreams. Perhaps you need to take classes to learn a new skill, or you may need to invest in tools or equipment.

The following worksheet, Action Steps to Your Goal, helps to define your obstacles and eliminate the things that are holding you back. Once obstacles are removed, you are free to enjoy the pursuit of your goals.

When planning your time and setting goals, consider what you can do to help your spouse and children meet their goals too.

ACTION STEPS TO YOUR GOAL

Goal: _____

What Bible Scripture encourages success to this goal? _____

_____

_____

_____

What are the personal benefits of reaching this goal? _____

_____

_____

_____

Who else will benefit when this goal is reached? _____

_____

_____

_____

Steps to Achieve Objective	Starting Date	Completion Date

What obstacles, delays, or resistance might you face when taking these steps toward your goal? What is the solution?

Obstacle:	Solution:

Actual Results:

_____

_____

_____

THE WORKING MOTHER'S COMMITMENT TO EXCELLENCE

I, _____,

commit to:

give when it is time to be a mother,

receive when I need a friend or neighbor,

understand when perspective can set me free,

believe when it's time to trust God, instead of me.

Signed _____

ABOUT THE AUTHORS

Cristine Bolley is a wife, mother, manager, editor, motivational speaker and writer who would rather watch birds with her daughters while drinking tea in her garden than tackle the carefully organized list of things to do in her daily planner. But she limits her tea drinking to Saturdays in the spring and the autumn because she enjoys checking off her lists.

With over twenty-five years of corporate communications and management experience, Cris is now a consulting director in an Executive Management Group which is responsible for several entrepreneurial enterprises in Tulsa, Oklahoma. She is also the Chief Editor of Honor Books. As an editorial director and acquisition editor, she has developed and ghostwritten numerous books over the past ten years.

Cris frequently teaches international writers' workshops and womens' conferences. Cris and her husband, Jim, lived in New Zealand for three years (where she developed her taste for tea) while working for an evangelical missionary organization. They now reside in Tulsa with their three beautiful daughters, Lindsey, Erin and Jamie.

Joann Cole Webster is a wife, mother of two sons, writer, editor and summa cum laude graduate of Southern California College who would rather not make a list of things to do in order get right to the task at hand while working out on her treadmill, watching the news, eating sushi, and listening to a cassette tape on how to do more in less time.

For nearly twenty years, Joann has worked with her father, Edwin Louis Cole, to establish the Christian Men's Global Network where she has worked her way to the position of Vice President. Her fast pace explains how she has managed at the same time to assist in the writing of many books, including, *Courage, Strong Men in Tough Times, Tapestry of Life I and II, We've Come a Long Way Baby, So Where Do We Go From Here?* and *Victory,* by A.C. Green.

Joann lived in Japan (where she acquired her taste for sushi) as a missionary for an interdenominational mission group and presently serves on the Board of Directors of God's House of Prayer, a fifty-year church-planting organization. She now lives in Dallas, Texas with her husband, Richard, and they enjoy the occasional longer-than-expected visits from one or both of their two grown sons, Josh and Seth.

Joann says that Cris has too many antiques in her house that require dusting, and Cris says Joann has too many responsibilities with twenty-four hour deadlines. During their ten-year friendship, they have discovered how their differences complement each other. Both women agree that it is possible to balance their many interests, responsibilities and dreams, while enjoying their various roles as women. While writing together they confirmed their theory that there are many ways to achieve more with less guilt and still build happier, healthier families.

Additional copies of this book and other
Honor Book titles of particular interest to women
are available at your local bookstore.

God's Little Instruction Book for Women by Honor Books
God's Little Instruction Book for Moms by Honor Books
God's Little Instruction Book for Couples by Honor Books
God's Little Devotional Book for Women by Honor Books
God's Little Devotional Book for Moms by Honor Books
God's Little Devotional Book for Couples by Honor Books
Tapestry of Life 1 and 2 by Nancy Corbett Cole
The Unique Woman by Edwin Louis Cole and Nancy Corbett Cole
Straight from the Heart for Mom by Richard Exley
One-Minute Businesswoman's Devotional by Mike Murdock
The Mother's Topical Bible by Honor Books